JUDICIOUS
DISCIPLINE

by
Forrest Gathercoal

Second Edition
revised and expanded

Judicious Discipline
By Forrest Gathercoal
Second Edition, 1990: Revised and Expanded

Copyright 1990 by Forrest Gathercoal

Published by **Caddo Gap Press**
    317 South Division Street, Suite 2
    Ann Arbor, Michigan 48104

Price - $9.95

ISBN 0-9625945-0-4
Library of Congress Catalog Card Number 90-080350

First Edition, 1987
Published by Prakken Publications, Inc.

Cover drawing by Brynn Lawler

Caddo Gap Press

Contents

Part III
The Balance: Synthesis and Evaluation   61

Part IV
Ethics: Beyond the Balance   119

Bibliography, Resources, and References   133

Acknowledgments

I wish to gratefully acknowledge and express my appreciation for the efforts of Barbara McEwan, Ed.D., and Kenneth Ahrendt, Ed.D., for their editorial assistance; Barbara McEwan, Ed.D., and Robert Bolden, Ph.D., for their research on *Judicious Discipline*; Margaret Abbott, Dan Anstine, Jerry Balaban, Glenn Gwynn, Kenneth Haines, Ken Hill, Richard Jensen, Paula Kinney, Jan Knight, Steve Mathews, Robert O'Neill, and Robert Payne, for their consultative assistance; and to Lucy Senter for her secretarial support; I also want to thank my dean, Robert Barr, Ph.D. for his continued help and encouragement. And finally to my family, teachers, students, and friends who have shared their lives with me--thanks for being there.

--**Forrest Gathercoal**

An uncomplicated, yet workable, rule has evolved from the classrooms of successful teachers throughout our country. Simply stated: "You may do what you want in this classroom until it interferes with the rights of others." It is their way of acknowledging individual differences among their students while recognizing the need for an educational environment free from disruptive forces. Teachers taking this position and applying it in an evenhanded manner to student conduct are unknowingly teaching and respecting their students' constitutional rights. And at the same time, they are creating a classroom environment in which students are able to learn about their responsibilities to the other members of the class.

Judicious Discipline, fashioned upon this principle, creates an educational and ethical perspective for school rules and decisions based on the *Bill of Rights*. By teaching students their citizenship rights, providing them an opportunity to experience individual liberties, and helping them understand the needs and demands of their social responsibilities, we are empowering students to govern and think for themselves. Educators have always believed teaching citizenship is an important aspect of their educational mission. *Judicious Discipline*, however, takes that belief one step further--to acknowledge and accept students as citizens. This democratic setting in our schools and classrooms serves to model the same system of laws under which students will live when their compulsory schooling is completed.

The book is divided into four parts:

Part I: **The Fulcrum: A Legal Perspective.** This provides a brief review of the historical background used in preparing this book and of the law applicable to public education. It is the foundation and framework for implementation of reasonable rules and decisions.

Part II: **The Fulcrum in Practice: An Educational Perspective.** This section introduces and supports an educational model for student discipline as opposed to a punishment approach to control students' behavior. Part II suggests a methodology for helping students learn and experience their individual rights as well as their responsibilities to others. It also serves as a guide for educators to develop school rules and consequences designed to create and maintain a democratic school environment.

Part III: **The Balance: Synthesis and Evaluation.** The importance of balancing the individual rights and educational needs of one student against the compelling interests of the majority is set out in the third section. Offered are strategies and techniques educators will find useful for the implementation of *Judicious Discipline*. In short, it is a wellspring from which teachers and administrators can draw as they formulate their own rules and related decisions accordant with their special needs and problems. The balance is not meant to be all inclusive of disciplinary and educational issues facing educators, but contains representative examples of school policies and procedures which affect student rights and responsibilities in the public school environment.

Part IV: **Ethics: Beyond the Balance**. This section examines professional responsibility and style, and functions as the conscience of student discipline by suggesting methods to create and maintain a professional relationship between student and educator.

In summary, *Judicious Discipline* is a disciplinary style and philosophy based on the synthesis of law, education, and ethics. In this book I bring together for the first time legal, educational, and ethical concepts designed as a framework to help educators examine all sides of educational and disciplinary issues. Although most educators will agree that the answers to everyday discipline problems cannot be quantified into a single publication, a disciplinary philosophy can be learned and developed which will reduce the complexities of the sundry daily decisions facing educators today.

Part I

The Fulcrum: A Legal Perspective

How often, in the faculty lounge, lunch room, and educational seminars do teachers and administrators express frustration over the plethora of legal issues they are required to understand and implement? This feeling of futility is often attributed to a national shift from the parental protectiveness of "in loco parentis," a legal phrase meaning the school stands in the place of a parent, to the realization that students "no longer shed their constitutional rights at the school house gate." It may be frustrating and time consuming for many of us to make the change from a parental approach of disciplining students to a more judicious approach that respects students as "young citizens." Now that public school students are legally "persons" within the meaning of our constitution, it is essential that teachers and administrators in public education today learn both the new language of the law and understand how it applies to the school setting. In other words, our schools and classrooms today are microcosms of the United States of America.

This point is brought home when students and parents confront educators with the statement, "You can't do that to me, I've got my rights." Asked to explain what they mean by their rights, most respond by saying, "I don't know, but I've got my rights." Although many use the phrase, few really understand its actual meaning.

The purpose of Part I is to help educators learn to speak and act with self-assurance on the subject of student rights. It provides a brief review of the historical background and the constitutional law applicable to public education. The Fulcrum, therefore, functions as the legal basis of a judicious model for student discipline.

The Democratic System

Students will graduate into a system of constitutional government which not only provides for the needs, interests, and welfare of the majority but bestows specific freedoms on each individual. Individual rights are not guaranteed, but neither are they easily denied by the majority. Growing up in America, most of us learned that democracy is a system of government in which the majority rules. We used this to settle playground arguments by voting on what game to play or seeking a consensus on the rules. Listening to students today, we realize this has not changed. Students continue to learn the concept of "the majority rules," but seldom in their schooling do they learn what it means or have an opportunity to experience the freedoms and responsibilities of **individual rights**. It is important that students learn that in our constitutional democracy individual rights are equally as important as the needs and interests of the majority.

The Bill of Rights

American constitutional liberties spring from the first ten amendments, better known as the *Bill of Rights*. The First Amendment's use of the term "freedom" in the context of religion, speech, press, and assembly is generally considered to be the most important amendment to the *Constitution*. The clauses "due process of law" in the Fifth and Fourteenth Amendments and "equal protection" in the Fourteenth Amendment are also significant and subject to widespread use and application in civil rights issues. Constitutional clauses are not self explanatory. Their meaning is translated into political, legal, and educational reality largely by the Supreme Court of the United States.

Constitutional rights exist to protect three basic values: freedom, justice, and equality. To live in a free society, however, does not mean we have license to do as we please. The controversy over the question of how, when, and where to limit individual **freedoms** is a never-ending question our society constantly seeks to balance. The difficulty lies in devising a precise formula to indicate when freedom has exceeded rightful bounds. **Justice** is concerned with due process and deals with basic governmental fairness. Many not familiar with the law question our justice system when they read or hear about a criminal being set free or an innocent person sent to prison. An analogy, however, can be drawn between the nation's justice system and our educational system, one which is designed to help students learn, but is also not entirely successful. We all are aware that both systems are well-conceived, yet occasionally fail and simply are not equal to the task in every case. Finally, **equality** presents us with the problem of distributing burdens and benefits. The proposition that "all people are created equal," has never meant that we all possess the same abilities, interests, or talents. These three values--freedom, justice and equality--have their antecedents in the United States *Constitution* and are basic to understanding individual liberties and civil rights.

⚖️

Student Rights

Students who say, "I've got my rights," are for the most part referring to the First, Fourth, and Fourteenth Amendments. Although other amendments and legislatively enacted laws are applicable to student learning and behavior, educators knowledgeable regarding these three amendments have a solid foundation when "talking about rights."

The First Amendment

> Congress shall make no law respecting an establishment of religion or prohibiting the free exercise thereof; or abridging the freedom of speech or of the press; or of the people peaceably to assemble, and to petition the government for a redress of grievances.

The First Amendment was designed to insure certain basic personal freedoms, which until 1969 were seldom applied to students in American public schools. However, in recent years numerous judicial decisions related to matters concerning free speech have been litigated. Freedom of the press has also generated considerable litigation concerning student rights to publish and distribute material on school premises. Furthermore, the two clauses in the First Amendment which relate to religion continue to have considerable impact on public educational programs. Of all the articles and amendments in the *Bill of Rights*, those related to church-state relationships have been the most difficult to litigate and apply to our school system. The court's adjudication of this provision has left teachers and administrators with considerable latitude for their own interpretations. As a result, a certain amount of subtle and unintentional discrimination remains in many public schools today.

The Fourth Amendment

> The right of the people to be secure in their
> persons, houses, papers, and effects, against
> unreasonable searches and seizures, shall not be
> violated, and no warrants shall issue, but upon
> probable cause, supported by oath or affirma-
> tion, and particularly describing the place to be
> searched, and the persons or things to be
> seized.

This amendment presents an issue of practical importance to all teachers and administrators who contemplate the search of student property such as lockers, purses, pockets, or student vehicles in the parking lot. Most faculty do not consider themselves to have the same societal charge as that of law enforcement officers. However, effective school discipline and management often require educators to use similar guidelines when taking property from students.

The Fourteenth Amendment

> All persons born or naturalized in the United
> States, and subject to the jurisdiction thereof,
> are citizens of the United States and of the
> State wherein they reside. No State shall make
> or enforce any law which shall abridge the
> privileges or immunities of citizens of the
> United States; **nor shall any State deprive any
> person of life, liberty, or property, without due
> process of law; nor deny to any person within
> its jurisdiction the equal protection of the laws.**

The last two clauses of the Fourteenth Amendment have had significant impact on public education. The first of these, known as the **due process** clause, provides the legal basis for rules which deny a student's access to education and extends from time spent in the hallway to expulsion from school. The last clause, known as the **equal protection** clause, serves as the constitutional foundation for all our laws and rules prohibiting discrimination. This clause is broadly interpreted in cases dealing with all forms of discrimination including sex, race, national origin, handicaps, marital status, age, and religion, and assures an equal educational opportunity for all students. In short, the Fourteenth Amendment acts as the fulcrum, allowing this fragile constitutional form of government to balance the countless needs and desires of individuals in our culturally rich and diverse society. Understanding educators able to apply the concepts of due process are usually perceived as possessing a sense of fairness and equality. Because of its importance, the next several pages are devoted to further explain the concepts of due process.

⚖️

Due Process

...nor shall any State deprive any person of life,
liberty or property, without the process of law;...

Picture the blindfolded woman symbolizing justice standing strong and confident, adorning the thresholds of our country's courthouses, her outstretched arm holding the familiar scales of justice. Imagine one scale heaped to the brim with the bodies of all the boys and girls in a public school actively engaged in their studies and activities. On the other side of the scale, picture one lone student, standing with book and sack lunch in hand, gazing apprehensively at the agglomeration of students amassed on the other side. This graphic illustration depicted on the cover of *Judicious Discipline* symbolizes the essence of "due process" as applied to our public schools.

In its simplest terms, due process is a legal effort to balance individual rights with the need to protect the welfare and interests of society. Only when the state is able to show a compelling reason why public welfare should weigh more than individual rights, will the court's scale of justice swing toward the mass of bodies. Conversely, if the government cannot demonstrate a **compelling state interest** then the rights of a single student will weigh more heavily than all who crowd the other side of the scale. As the scales of justice tip in favor of the minority, it is incumbent upon the majority to respect and show consideration for that individual's rights.

Although succinct, the due process clause represents two hundred years of common law application and thousands of court decisions clarifying and interpreting its meaning. To fully understand and appreciate the complexity of this constitutional concept, we must first begin by examining the clause a few words at a time.

"...nor shall any State" means that in order to have a right to due process there must be state action. When applied to education, only students and faculty in **public** schools enjoy due process rights; their counterparts in our nation's private schools do not. The legal rights of students and faculty in private schools are expressly set out in the contract between individuals and the private corporation which usually administers the school. Dismissal from a private school would therefore be considered a breach of contract by the non-conforming student. Students who disobey or are not satisfied with the rules of a private school are free to choose another school. Conversely, compulsory attendance laws and public funding combine to create the state action necessary for students' rights to due process in public schools.

"...deprive any person" means withholding these constitutional rights from any person within the jurisdiction of the United States, both citizens and non-citizens. The law has been extended to include those non-citizens who are in the United States illegally. This is not to say that illegal aliens have a right to live here, but they do have the right to due process while living here, including the right to legal proceedings which may lead to their deportation. "Any person" is broadly interpreted by the courts and today includes students in our public schools.

"**...of life, liberty, or property**" defines those rights which may be deprived through due process by governmental action. It is interesting to note that the framers of our *Constitution* used just three words to protect our past, present, future, and even death at the hands of the government. For example, the word "**property**" includes everything a person legally owns and has acquired up to the present. It covers such tangible properties as real estate, personal property, and money, as well as intangibles like contracts of employment, eligibility and entitlement to welfare payments, and the right of students to attend public schools.

The second word "**liberty**" begins with the present and embodies all future acquisitions and aspirations.

> ...it denotes not merely freedom from bodily restraint but also the right of the individual to contract, to engage in any of the common occupations of life, to acquire useful knowledge, to marry, establish a home and bring up children, to worship God according to the dictates of his own conscience, and generally to enjoy those privileges long recognized...as essential to the orderly pursuit of happiness by free men. *Meyer v. Nebraska* (262 US 390, 399; 1923).

Too often the liberty issue is overlooked for the more understood and simpler applied property aspect. The sections in this book on Grading Practices and Compulsory School Attendance offer good examples of liberty as it applies to the public school setting. Educators devoted to helping students succeed, and who sincerely care about their future opportunities, exemplify the importance of liberty within the meaning and spirit of constitutional rights and, as a result, often enjoy a special place as a role model and mentor to their students.

Finally, the word "**life**" refers to the loss of personal life at the hands of the government, such as the execution of a criminal.

Stated in positive terms, the government may deprive a person of life, liberty, or property only if the individual is given due process.

"**...without due process of law**" means the process due persons by the local, state, and federal governments. Clarifying its application to everyday situations, court decisions have separated "due process" into two distinct aspects: **substantive** and **procedural**.

"**Substantive**" **due process** pertains to the legislation, the rule, or the law itself, and means a basic fairness in the substance of the decision. If the state attempted to deprive a person of life, liberty, or property, substantive due process would require a valid objective and means that are reasonably calculated to achieve the objective. The rule should:

1. Have some rational need for its adoption;
2. Be as good in meeting the need as any alternative that reasonable people would have developed;
3. Be supported by relevant and substantial evidence and findings of fact.

In other words, substantive due process implies that laws and decisions must be legal before our government can deprive someone of their life, liberty, or property. Whenever someone questions a rule or seeks clarification of a decision, that individual is legally exercising their Fourteenth Amendment **substantive** due process rights.

"**Procedural**" **due process** relates to the decision-making process used when determining whether a rule or law has been violated. Basic fairness in adjudication is required and has been interpreted by the courts to include the following:

1. Adequate notice.
2. A fair and impartial hearing.
3. The right to appeal the decision.

Adequate notice includes such procedures as charges, evidence to be used against the person charged, a reasonable amount of time to prepare a defense, the time and place of the hearing, and adequacy of form (oral and written). **A fair and impartial hearing** encompasses elements such as a meaningful opportunity to be heard, state a position, and present witnesses. It also may include the right to counsel, presentation and cross-examination of witnesses, and review written reports in advance of the hearing. **The right of appeal** is not only applicable to our state and federal court system, but is an integral part of our governmental structure as well.

With few exceptions, the Due Process Clause allows all administrative interpretations and decisions, as well as the rule in question, to be appealed through a school district's administrative structure. From the school district, the decision or rule may be appealed to a higher state or federal administrative agency and then referred to an appropriate court. Every rule or decision made in public schools is subject to review by another person, board, or court. An educator who says, "This is a non-appealable decision" is bluffing. Most are unaware students have this right of appeal and that it is possible for their decision or rule to someday reach the United States Supreme Court. Due process, as is the case with many legal concepts, resists a simple dictionary definition and tends to be a dynamic rather than a static concept.

Other Amendments

Although the First, Fourth and Fourteenth Amendments are most often cited, some familiarity with the Fifth, Eighth, Ninth, and Tenth Amendments could be helpful. The self-incrimination clause of the **Fifth Amendment** has been employed by teachers questioned about their activities outside the classroom. It is only applicable in questions of criminal activity and, therefore, not relevant in most school situations. The just compensation clause of the Fifth Amendment is used occasionally in educational litigation to protect citizens' rights to just compensation when property is appropriated for school purposes.

The **Eighth Amendment** prohibits excessive bail and fines

and protects citizens from cruel and unusual punishment. While this amendment has appeared more often in suits challenging the treatment of prisoners or other persons involuntarily institutionalized, it has been used in a few cases to protest the use of corporal punishment in public schools. Such challenges have generally favored the schools, therefore prompting most parents to sue in tort for money damages against injuries caused by excessive physical punishment.

The **Ninth Amendment** stipulates that the rights enumerated in the United States *Constitution* shall not be construed to deny or disparage other rights retained by the people. This amendment supports other freedom arguments and has appeared in educational litigation dealing with the assertion of rights to personal privacy by students and teachers. It has also been successfully interwoven with other amendments that provide for our basic personal freedoms.

The **Tenth Amendment**, often referred to as the reserved-powers clause, states; "The powers not delegated to the United States by the *Constitution*, nor prohibited by it to the States, are reserved to the States respectively, of the people." The United States *Constitution* does not provide a legal base for public education in America. Hence, this amendment has been the underpinning for any state assuming the primary responsibility for education. Our Federal *Constitution*, however, is the source of all of our nation's laws and generally supersedes state law wherever there is a direct conflict between Federal and State governments.

A Pocket-Sized

History of School Rules

Until 1969, court decisions historically supported the concept of *in loco parentis*, which granted to the schools the same legal authority over students as that of a parent. In the absence of "state action," implicit in the Fourteenth Amendment, children who live with parents or legal guardians enjoy no constitutional rights. For example, parents searching their daughter's bedroom without a search warrant, would not violate her Fourth Amendment rights from unreasonable search or seizure, or a son denied the keys to the car would have no Fourteenth Amendment right to appeal his parents' decision. *In loco parentis* allowed schools ultimate authority, provided rules were not unreasonable, capricious, arbitrary, malicious, or made in bad faith. For years, this concept fostered a commonly accepted practice of upholding rules that mirrored the thinking, customs, and discipline found in most American homes.

There is legislation, however, that protects children from their parents and legal guardians. State child-abuse laws and federal child-labor legislation are two examples of society's means of safeguarding children from abusive parental acts. Early court decisions applied this "abuse test" to protect students in public schools, but unless the rule or decision was clearly abusive, courts would not intercede. The law presumed professional educators were more knowledgeable about matters of student development and discipline than judges and juries of townspeople. Parents' knowledge that they carried the burden of proof and fear of retaliatory acts against their children prevented most from seeking redress in court. However, in situations where parents did sue for relief, school districts generally prevailed.

Today, courts rarely use the concept **in loco parentis** when writing opinions on student issues. This concept has been replaced by language which addresses the constitutional rights and responsibilities of students. Although there have been prior questions considered, the *Tinker v. Des Moines Independent School District* (393 U.S. 503) case in 1969 was the first United States Supreme Court decision in the general area of student discipline. The case, cited ritualistically by school authorities as well as student plaintiffs, establishes general guidelines applicable to many school situations. This landmark case involved high school students suspended by their principal for wearing black arm bands to school protesting the United States' involvement in Vietnam. The students won the right to express their political beliefs when the court stated for the first time:

> ...First Amendment rights, applied in light of the special characteristics of the school environment, are available to teachers and students. It can hardly be argued that either students or teachers shed their constitutional rights to freedom of speech or expression at the schoolhouse gate...

It is apparent that times have changed from the days when school rules resembled those used in most families. Today, the rules school authorities use must recognize and take into consideration the constitutional rights of students. If, in fact, students do not shed their constitutional rights at the gate, a graphic illustration of the *Tinker* decision might be to imagine students dressing each morning in attire selected from their wardrobe of liberties. By the time they have donned their mail of "freedom," buckled on a sword of "justice," and grasped the shield of "equality," they will look like knights of King Arthur's Round Table in full battle dress, as they walk through the schoolhouse gate. This is truly a formidable image for any teacher to confront each day. To complicate matters, frustrated teachers and administrators are frequently heard to say, "The students have more rights than I have."

We are now at the core, the very heart and soul of the question facing educators in public schools today. **Is there a way to establish and maintain an effective learning environment in our schools, while teaching and respecting student rights of freedom, justice, and equality?**

As foreboding as recognizing and respecting students' constitutional rights appear at first blush, there is another side to the scale of justice. There are, in fact, four sagacious and time-tested public interest arguments crafted in the courts and construed for the precise purpose of limiting constitutionally protected freedoms. These arguments are as genuine and well-grounded in legal principle and history as the line of reasoning which allows for individual rights. This legal concept is commonly referred to as a **"compelling state interest"** and simply means that in some cases the needs and interests of the majority weigh greater than those of an individual--any individual. One of the distinguishing characteristics of *Judicious Discipline* is that it helps students understand and appreciate society's desideratum and its applicability to the public school environs.

⚖

Compelling State Interest

Prior to the 1970s, when a teacher was asked by a student to explain the reason for a rule, the teacher's response would have been: "Because I am your teacher and this is the way we have always done it" or "You will have to learn to follow rules someday so you might as well learn to follow mine." This response is known as a rule for rules' sake and is much like a parent's response to the same question. Today, however, the burden of proof that a school rule is legal is incumbent upon the educators responsible for promulgating the rule. A student today questioning the reason for a rule might hear the response: "Let me tell you my compelling state interest for the rule." Although the rule may be the same in both situations, the language and educational posture has changed substantially.

The legality of a school rule is generally presumed, and the burden of proof rests on the complaining student. However, if a rule actually infringes on a fundamental constitutional right, the burden of proof then shifts to school officials to demonstrate a compelling state need. The closer laws come to encroaching on student substantive rights, the greater the need for justification and clarification by school authorities. For example, the need to maintain a proper learning environment is a compelling state interest which allows school boards to legally prohibit conduct detrimental to the operation of schools. Therefore, a rule which deprives a student of substantive or procedural due process rights must be directly related to the welfare of the school.

Now that it is clear educators must have a compelling state interest to sustain their rules and decisions, this begs the question: **What are these compelling state interests?** For years our nation's courts have been using four basic arguments in an effort to sustain the balance between the individual and state interest in our public schools. These compelling state interests are:

1. Property loss or damage.
2. Legitimate educational purpose.
3. Health and safety.
4. Serious disruption of the educational process:
    a. What is serious?
    b. Must the disruption have already occurred or is the threat of a disruption enough to sustain the rule or decision?
    c. For whom should the rule be intended, the individual who is exercising constitutional rights or the majority who are disquieted or inconvenienced by the individual's exercise of those rights?

School rules and decisions based on these four compelling state interest arguments will, in all probability, withstand the test of today's court rulings despite the fact that they deny students their individual rights. Teachers and administrators not only have a legal right to deny student constitutional rights, but it is their professional responsibility to prohibit student behaviors when the exercise of those rights seriously affects the welfare of the school. It is clearly the school official's duty as an officer of the state to maintain a safe and proper educational environment.

Property Loss or Damage

"Wear appropriate shoes on the gym floor."
"Respect the property of others."
*"Return the athletic equipment after you play with
    it."*

Care of property is usually an easy concept for students to understand and few argue their right to damage school facilities or take the property of others. However, twelve years of public schooling provides students many opportunities to remove or perhaps damage state-owned property as well as the property of other students. Taxpayers, therefore, rely heavily on the sound judgment of teachers and administrators to oversee the care and maintenance of public property entrusted to them. Further, parents and guardians also depend on school personnel to assist in protecting their children's property within the jurisdiction of school authority. Rules must be explicit, fair, and reasonably related to the loss or damage intended to be prevented in order to insure adequate notice.

Legitimate Educational Purpose

*"It is compulsory for all school-age children to
    attend school."*
"Bring your school supplies and books to class."
*"Our lesson today is the correct use of pro-
    nouns."*

The public mandates teachers and administrators maintain instructional programs consistent with state law. They are considered the experts in matters of academic decisions which include content, rigor, and student achievement. Plagiarism, classroom and homework assignments, grading systems, special or advanced placement, and other school decisions and proce-dures which are designed to enhance students' learning and achievement are illustrations of the scope of this compelling state interest. Courts are reluctant to second-guess educational or curricular decisions based on sound professional judgment. However, some cases involving the school's conflicts with family values will tip the scales in favor of individual rights, such as students being excused from classes teaching evolution. Generally speaking, all policies and decisions having a tenable educational motive related to appropriate school objectives come within the intent of this standard. As students obtain jobs or deal with governmental agencies, legitimate educational purpose becomes legitimate employer purpose or, when dealing with law enforcement, legitimate police purpose. This is a reasonable analogy to use when students and parents object to educational rules and decisions.

Threat to Health and Safety

> *"Move carefully in the halls."*
> *"Behave safely toward others."*
> *"Students must have proof of vaccinations before registering for school."*

A fundamental purpose of government is to protect the health and welfare of its citizens and, especially, students who attend America's public schools. Courts consistently sustain rules and decisions designed to maintain the health and safety of the majority and are quick to deny individual freedoms in such matters.

The importance of health and safety rules is apparent in school situations which expose students to the dangers of playgrounds, shops, science labs, physical education, and sports. Although students may complain about rules which prohibit rough play or require the use of protective equipment, school authorities must deny student rights to insure the health and safety of themselves and others. If student rights are on a collision course with a potential student injury, the decision must be in the school's favor. Students will receive lifetime benefits from exemplary health and safety programs if rules concerned with their welfare are all inclusive, conspicuous, and rigorously enforced.

▓▓▓▓▓▓Serious Disruption of the Educational Process

> *"No gang activity on school premises."*
> *"Keep your hands and feet to yourself."*
> *"Language and dress must be appropriate for the school environment."*

The establishment and enforcement of rules that foster and encourage a proper educational environment are necessary to the efficient and successful operation of every school. School officials have both the legal authority and the professional responsibility to deny student rights which seriously disrupt student activities. At first glance, "serious disruption" may appear to be uncomplicated and easily defined. However, consideration must be given to three very important questions that need to be carefully weighed before a judicious decision can be rendered.

What is serious? The language of today's courts stipulates that: "the disruption must materially and/or substantially interfere with the requirements of appropriate discipline in the operation of the public schools." Each situation must be decided on its own merits and may vary from one classroom to another in the same building. For example, the acceptable hubbub of a craft class could or could not be a serious disruption in a social studies class, depending on teaching style and educational purpose.

The Supreme Court in the *Tinker* case considered closely whether students wearing black armbands to school did or did not seriously disrupt the student body. The Court stated:

> Only a few of the 18,000 students in the school
> system wore the black armbands. Only five

students were suspended for wearing them.
There is no indication that the work of the
school or any class was disrupted. Outside the
classrooms, a few students made hostile remarks to the children wearing armbands, but
there were no threats or acts of violence on
school premises. In order for the State in the
person of school officials to justify prohibition
of a particular expression of opinion, it must be
able to show that its action was caused by
something more than a mere desire to avoid the
discomfort and unpleasantness that always
accompany an unpopular viewpoint.

It is important to note the last sentence of the court's ruling,
because it gives us some sense of "what is serious." Apparently
"serious" means more than just actions and expressions which
are unpleasant or make educators and others feel uncomfortable.
If the act or expression is a serious disruption, the students'
rights will give way to society's expectations. If it is not serious,
educators can help an inconvenienced or annoyed majority
understand and appreciate the value of and reasons for individual
rights.

Must the serious disruption have already occurred, or is the
threat of a serious disruption enough to sustain the rule or
decision? Again, we turn to the words of the *Tinker* decision for
guidance:

...in our system, undifferentiated fear or ap-
prehension of disturbance is not enough to
overcome the right to freedom of expression.
Any departure from absolute regimentation may
cause trouble. Any variation from the majority's
opinion may inspire fear. Any word spoken, in
class, in the lunchroom or on the campus, that
deviates from the views of another person, may
start an argument or cause a disturbance. But
our *Constitution* says we must take this risk; and

our history says that it is this sort of hazardous
freedom--this kind of openness--that is the basis
of our national strength and of the indepen-
dence and vigor of Americans who grow up and
live in the relatively permissive, often dis-
putatious society.

Often rules and decisions are based on the fear that something may occur when, in fact, it may never have happened and is
not likely to happen. This, of course, varies greatly from one
situation to another and could make congruous decisions difficult. The fact that the school board bears the burden of proof
as to whether or not the wearing of armbands "...might reasonably have led school authorities to forecast substantial disruption..." also compounds the issue. To what extent should a school
board be permitted to adopt preventive rules and when is it
required to wait "until the horse is stolen before locking the barn
door?" This is a most difficult question, yet one which administrators and teachers must resolve daily. Educators concerned about student rights must seek out and obtain the best
information and advice available, balance this knowledge in the
context of both their duty to the state and to individual rights,
and resolve it with a "best effort" decision. Although possibly
disgruntled by the decision, those affected will appreciate the
thoughtful consideration and professional demeanor exhibited by
the process.

For whom should the rule be intended: the individual who
is exercising constitutional rights or the majority who are dis-
quieted or inconvenienced by the individual's exercise of those
rights? Shortly after the Beatles made their first appearance on
the *Ed Sullivan Show* in the 1960s, some boys began to wear
their hair over their ears, then below their collars, and eventually
down their backs. They were often taunted by other boys and
occasionally pushed into a girl's restroom or sometimes caught
in a little-used hallway and given a haircut. Most principals
faulted the boys with long hair for causing the disruptions and
usually suspended them until they cut their hair. Punishing the

small number of students deviating from the norm was a common solution to the problem at that time. Only a few administrators, who believed hair styles represented a student's right of free speech and expression, considered suspending the harassing students. Against whom should you direct your rule, those exercising their rights or those exercised by their exercise? The *Tinker* decision helps clarify the issue:

> Students in school as well as out of school are "persons" under our *Constitution*. They are possessed of fundamental rights which the State must respect, just as they themselves must respect their obligations to the State. Judge Gewin, speaking for the Fifth Circuit, said that school officials cannot suppress expressions of feelings with which they do not wish to contend.

Although it may be administratively more convenient to threaten suspension of a few students rather than suffering through the inconvenience and unpopularity associated with helping the majority understand, teachers and administrators today should assume a leadership role and hold themselves accountable for safeguarding individual student rights.

Students must understand that their rights do not allow them to do as they please. Rights are quickly lost when their actions infringe on the property and well-being of others, or become a serious disruption of the educational process. There is, as well, a professional responsibility on the part of teachers and administrators to carefully weigh student human rights as they bring about the educational equanimity envisioned by America's public. This is not easily accomplished. Balancing the obligation to provide for the liberties of a single student with the pressures brought about by the clamor of the majority can add up to a lot of heat in the new schoolhouse kitchen. Because of the thin line educators must tread, there may well be a need to view rules and decisions from a constitutional perspective in order to provide a well-regulated and orderly climate for learning.

Part II

The Fulcrum in Practice: An Educational Perspective

One of our educational system's more glaring contradictions is the autocratic public school system we use as a model for teaching students to be responsible citizens in a democratic society. Ironically, the first personal involvement most children experience with government is when they are compelled to schooling by state compulsory education laws. They are forced into a system of rules and decisions not unlike the authority they encounter at home, an authority which rewards obedience, punishes offenders, and needs no justification other than "I am your parent." It is no surprise that parents and teachers continually ask children, "When are you going to grow up and begin thinking for yourself?" If the management system in our public schools parallels the autocratic environment of most American homes, it follows that educators may be preparing graduates who are unable to understand or function well in a participatory society. Many who have tried have found that in the long run the benefits of enabling students to think as and act like responsible citizens far outweigh the disciplinary expediency of teaching blind obedience.

Part II develops a framework of school rules and consequences designed to alleviate this dichotomy between schools and society at large. The Fulcrum in Practice integrates our nation's laws with an educational model for teaching students about their individual rights and freedoms along with their responsibilities to others. In other words, *Judicious Discipline* uses "law and order" as an educational approach to student discipline. As a result, students will not only be regarded as citizens and learn to think for themselves in a democratic form of government, but have an opportunity to experience the joys and sorrows of being accountable for their own actions.

⚖️

The Perspective in Practice

As educators we must develop a new rationality if we are going to respect our students as citizens. This democratic mindset may be illustrated by using an example of a rule common to many classrooms. "No chewing gum" is a rule widely enforced and designed to keep gum from under desks and seats, out of hair and/or textbooks, from being popped or chewed noisily, and to prevent the litter of gum wrappers. Envision, if you will, a new student entering your classroom at mid-semester, wearing a three-piece suit, hand-made Italian shoes, carrying a brief case and portable lap-top computer, and chewing the biggest wad of gum you have ever seen. His admit slip indicates he is the sole heir of a family who are the principle shareholders in a vast chewing gum corporation. Inquiring about the gum in his mouth, you are told that he is simply carrying on a family tradition symbolic of their commitment to the idea that gum can be chewed properly and is acceptable in any social setting. In other words, in this scenario his chewing gum is a statement of personal belief and an expression of family values based on his First Amendment right of free speech.

Although the example exaggerates to emphasize a point, there may be a sound legal and rational basis for the student's argument. On the other hand, any one of the four compelling state interest arguments previously set out in Part I may weigh heavier than the personal expression of a single gum-chewer. Let's apply the state's rationale to a gum chewer's individual right of free expression.

First, **property damage** is the rationale commonly used to restrict gum chewing in class. However, this reasoning may break down if it is established that damage does not occur when students chew gum, but only when gum is out of their mouths. Perhaps the rule necessitates a place to hide gum and, therefore, the rule against chewing gum is the major cause of gum damage to school property. A better rule to protect property would be a rule prohibiting gum from being out of students' mouths unless wrapped in paper. **Legitimate educational purpose** would not be congruous unless one wanted to model the evils of chewing. Teaching the proper use of gum, however, would be more appropriate to educational purpose. **Health and safety** would be a good reason to teach the health advantages to sugarless gum or to enforce a rule against gum chewing during physical activities to prevent a student from choking. Specific rules against popping and chewing loudly should be enough to prevent a **serious disruption**.

Although this scenario may appear contrived, it gives us an example of how educators must approach rules and decisions. Promulgating rules today necessitates first considering the rights of the student--then weighing those rights with the state's four compelling interests. Teachers and administrators not only face the challenge of sustaining at least one of the four compelling state interests, but also must bear the burden of proof. If none of the four compelling state interests are reasonable or applicable, it would be advisable to back off and reconsider. One purposeless rule strictly enforced simply destroys administrative credibility and leaves suspect all other rules and subsequent decisions.

The Educational Model

Instead of using rules and punishments as a means of controlling gum activities, why not approach the matter as an educator would--**teach students how to use gum properly**. I am reminded of a workshop on student rights I recently presented to a group of school administrators and an anecdote an elementary principal shared with us about his experience with "the gum problem." He had been a teacher in his building before being appointed principal and was familiar with the problem they had with gum damage. The custodian was constantly complaining about the wrappers on the floor and gum under the furniture. The punishments for chewing gum were harsh, but the problem continued. When he became an administrator, one of his first acts was to revise some of the rules. One change in particular reversed the ban on gum chewing. The new plan suggested that the faculty spend some time during the first day of class teaching students how to use gum properly. Teachers instructed their classes in the appropriate way to chew gum, how to wrap it in paper when out of their mouths, where to discard the gum, and how to care for the empty wrapper. Curious about the effect of this educational approach, a few weeks into the school year, the principal asked the building custodian if there was a problem with gum in the building. The custodian replied that he was surprised by the fact there was no gum anywhere around school, not even wrappers on the floor. "I don't know what you did," he said, "but you are the toughest principal we ever had here." Another three weeks passed. The conversation again surfaced and still no evidence of gum damage was found. "You really are tough," the principal was told. "What did you do?" The principal explained that the old rules were replaced by a more positive educational approach to teaching responsibility. The custodian listened in disbelief and, without a word, walked away shaking his head.

Too often educators find themselves inventing an endless parade of rules hoping to create the illusion of being in control. Many are convinced it is rules and punishments which teach responsibility, or believe a "line in the dirt" approach to discipline is what children want. Once a teacher's line is crossed, however, the illusion of being in control begins to unravel. Until students are allowed to experience and begin to feel a proprietary interest in school and classroom rules, student control and a good learning environment will always be at risk. Teachers and administrators must move away from the appearance of a teacher-imposed "hard-line" method, to an educational approach emphasizing our skills and abilities as professional educators. We should focus our efforts on teaching and modeling the attitudes and behaviors appropriate to learning and good citizenship. Students are far more likely to develop good character and become accountable when they are provided an opportunity to learn and actively participate in a democratic learning environment. When they waiver from these judiciously imposed boundaries, they need an educator nearby, not a parent substitute or a quasi-law enforcement officer to pull them back into line. When an academic or behavior problem does occur it is an unswerving and dedicated educator who pauses to think--"What needs to be learned here?" Every student problem then becomes an educational challenge. How much more effective our schools could be if we would teach the rationale for society's boundaries and the value of compliance. Teachers and administrators must approach discipline as professional educators and do what they have prepared themselves to do, by finding ways to help students learn and develop the attitudes and knowledge necessary to live productively and responsibly in a democratic school setting.

⚖️

Judicious Model
Versus Punishment Model

When it comes to managing student behavioral problems, many educators believe a system of rewards and punishment best serves their professional needs. They argue the educational benefits of rewards outweigh the problems caused by punishing students. They feel, once the rules and consequences are established, their responsibility as educators is to be consistent as they play out their announced plan of action. Furthermore, they are convinced that to bend the rules or treat some students differently would not be fair to the others. The argument is often made that students know what the rules are and should not be surprised or even upset over paying the consequences for wrongdoing. This line of thinking leads these educators to conclude that punitive actions are what students will experience in the "real world" and that punishment, or the fear of punishment, teaches them to be responsible for their own actions.

Punishment models feed upon the appearance of justice and appear to be logical and work well with most students. Upon closer scrutiny, however, these models may actually be antithetical to our educational mission and professional objectives. An educational approach to behavioral problems is generally construed by students as positive and helpful to their needs, while punishment is perceived as negative and usually ends in an adversarial relationship. Many students who feel punished, regardless of the educator's intent, imitate that behavior and believe that they have license to reciprocate by punishing the educator back. This retaliatory urge sets in motion a negative attitude which stifles learning, dampens enthusiasm for school, and drives a wedge between student and educator. This failure of the all-important student/educator relationship leads almost immediately to an escalation of learning and behavioral problems. Students learn to fear or hate educators, subjects, and events that have been punishing. If the consequences of failing are too severe, students may learn to cheat, withdraw, skip classes, or drop out of school. When a student feels estranged from the student/educator relationship, the student loses an educator and often turns to others for support and learning, such as peers, gangs, or possibly misguided adults.

Whereas reinforcement is designed to strengthen behavior, punishment, on the other hand, is intended to suppress an undesired behavior. Although punishment may work to suppress one unwanted behavior, it often negatively affects other desired behaviors. I still remember the first time when I, as a beginning music teacher, decided to dramatically enforce the school's ban on gum chewing during the middle of a rehearsal. A trite and contrived lecture to the student about the evils of gum in school, followed by ordering the offending student to march to the waste basket and spit it out, took about two minutes of class time, but my thoughtless decision to "make an example" of a gum-chewing trombone player led to an immediate collapse of the remainder of our rehearsal. I will never forget my dismay at the disappearance of student enthusiasm and interest displayed just two minutes before. Intonation and dynamics were gone. I had the feeling students were patronizing me and we were all just going through the motions. Somehow I struggled through the rest of the period realizing what I had done. On my way home later that afternoon I remember saying to myself, "I'll never do that again." I then decided the maintenance of the educational environment had to be more important than punishing one student in front of the class for a rule infraction.

Many discipline models are more concerned with correcting deficiencies than developing and using strategies to change student goals. The student/educator relationship provides an excellent vehicle for helping students change as it brings into play the expertise and resources of many well-qualified communicators, counselors, advisors, mentors, role models, and personnel with patience, know-how, understanding, empathy, and an unyielding commitment to helping students. These resources must be directed more and more toward changing students' attitudes and keeping them in school. An educational relationship now begins to develop between teacher and student. The measure of student success in all likelihood will be directly related to the establishment and continuing professional association among educators, students, and their families.

If a judicious model is going to work, educators must have an understanding of human growth and development, learning theory, and classroom management, as well as skill and knowledge about how to motivate and encourage. If educators do not understand how students learn or why they behave as they do, it will be difficult for them to assist all of their students in the process of subject mastery or behavior change. And if educators are offended by certain student attitudes, they must begin by changing their mind-set before they can truly help those students. A discouraged or intolerant educator can seldom, if ever, encourage or motivate a student. Educators who have the ability and resourcefulness to help change student attitudes and clarify their goals are long remembered and play a significant part in the lives of young people.

There is a healing nature to a judicious model for student discipline from which "good vibes" seem to emanate. Constructive, positive, workable, enthusiastic ideas spring from the minds of educators focused on student learning. In addition to learning, these educators place great value on firm and fair rules and judicious consequences administered with reason and compassion. In many instances, professional educators may only be there to stop the bleeding and are seldom around to see the wounds heal. However, healing takes time and only now and then do educators experience the extrinsic rewards that are the benefits of a judicious model. We must be confident that education can bring about desired change in young people, or other models will appear more expedient and offer the illusion of immediate results. The intrinsic rewards of a job well-done have long been the acknowledged legacy of every professional practice.

⚖️

Formulating School Rules

▰▰▰▰*Legal Implications*

There are legal limits to the latitude of legislative authority school officials have when structuring rules appropriate to their teaching or administrative responsibility. A teacher, for example, may adopt any classroom rule so long as it does not violate the rules of the principal, superintendent, school board, and state department of education. The classroom, school, or district structure cannot subtend state and federal legislative laws, the weight of state and federal case authority, or the United States *Constitution*. These are "the givens"--rules that are already decided and, good or bad, must be followed.

Faced with all the legislative and administrative strata, a new teacher may feel at a loss trying to locate and assimilate all the pertinent laws. These established rules and regulations are available to educators through a number of official state publications. **First,** examine the state administrative laws affecting public education, available through state departments of education. These laws are most commonly referred to as state department administrative rules or codes. **Second,** investigate school board policies, usually available in the district office or school libraries. **Third,** if there is a negotiated collective bargaining agreement, know the rules agreed upon by the teachers and the school board. **Fourth,** read your principal's rules regarding building policies and regulations relating to teacher responsibilities. **Lastly,** review a copy of the student handbook and know the rules affecting students in your building. Know your boundaries and the rules you cannot change. It's hard to say this delicately, but violating your administrators' rules is known as insubordination.

A rule should first be written in broad general terms, inclusive enough to account for all possible student behaviors.

The four compelling state interests described previously provide a good outline to follow, and certainly meet the all-inclusive criteria. If, however, these four were the only rules, they would be unconstitutionally vague because of their breadth and, as a result, violate students' procedural due process rights to adequate notice. For instance, a rule preventing school property damage places students on notice not to destroy the school, but this rule is not specific enough as to what behavior would be injurious. It would not, for example, sufficiently inform students that the gym floor is more susceptible to damage from regular street shoes than the floors in the hallways and classrooms.

An initial broad heading should be followed by specific examples of student behavior. The list need not be exhaustive, but should encompass a number of examples to facilitate awareness and understanding of the rules. Include rules which were learned from past incidents and problem areas that could be reasonably anticipated.

Crystal Schmidt-Dipaola, principal at Minter Bridge Elementary School in Hillsboro, Oregon, recently appointed a building CORE Team representing each grade level to develop building rules based on *Judicious Discipline*. The Team came up with the following recommendations for the whole Minter Bridge community:

1. Act in a Safe and Healthy Way.

Use furniture appropriately, walk in the building and other designated areas, follow playground rules, follow bus riding rules, keep hands and feet to self. (Compelling State Interest: Health and Safety)

2. Treat All Property With Respect.

Take care of textbooks, library books, school furniture, school bathrooms, computers, and personal property of others. Borrow the property of others ONLY after asking permission. (Compelling State Interest: Property)

3. Respect the Rights and Needs of Others.

Work without disruption, show courtesy towards others, cooperate to help others learn, use appropriate language, feel good about yourselves. (Compelling State Interest: Serious Disruption of the Educational Process)

4. Take Responsibility for Learning.

Strive for excellence, work hard and do your best, come to school prepared to learn, be a good listener, turn in your assignments on time, do your homework, keep track of your materials, set a good example for others. (Compelling State Interest: Legitimate Educational Process)

Keep rules to a minimum. The four major headings followed by appropriate examples are easy for students to remember and educators to manage and enforce. This two-pronged approach will address students who argue, "The rules didn't cover that," as well as students who claim, "I didn't know what you meant." The law does not require school authorities to state all of the rules in writing before school begins in the fall. Courts will allow reasonable additions and deletions during the school year. The central question is whether the school can show cause for the rule change and whether students are given adequate notice. Any of the compelling state interests should withstand this test of reasonable cause.

Write rules explicitly and clearly for the educational level of those affected. It is imperative that students fully understand the meaning of rules in order to meet the notice requirement of the Fourteenth Amendment. "Ignorance of the law is no excuse," is a common phrase, but it has little application to school-aged children required to attend public schools under our compulsory education laws. Almost all are minors, some with limited English-speaking ability, while others may be handicapped. Merely giving students a copy of the school and classroom rules or posting them is not sufficient notice in some cases to allow legal enforcement.

Policy Considerations

Equally important as the legality of school rules is the message they communicate to students and parents about how students will be valued. The student handbook and respective classroom rules are, for most parents and students, a first impression of the resolve and compassion of their school's environment. Rules that generate a positive feeling of student support help alleviate the fears and belligerence attributed to anticipated encounters many have with stereotyped authority figures.

By using some of the language from *Judicious Discipline*, the teachers and administrators of Cleveland High School in Portland, Oregon, composed the following statement of philosophy to be used as a preamble to their student handbook. It reads as follows:

> Cleveland High School is a learning environment in which members of this community feel comfortable, challenged, and involved. The members of the Cleveland community are responsible to each other for behavior that exhibits an awareness of respect for human dignity and individual differences. Members of this community share the responsibility to maintain a safe climate that promotes and encourages learning.
>
> As members of this community, students have the right to know the rationale for the rules and decisions affecting them, a right to an equal educational opportunity, and an opportunity to participate in the procedures which ensure these rights. Students will lose these rights when their individual actions infringe on the rights or property of others.
>
> The primary goal of Cleveland High School is to prepare students to be contributing members of a society which uses a democratic process. Ultimately, Cleveland graduates will possess academic and social skills that will prepare them to function as responsible citizens.

The building rules that follow this preamble, as well as each teacher's classroom rules, reflect this building philosophy. The principal, Robert O'Neill, also plans to use this statement as a basis for hiring new teachers, as well as evaluating present staff members.

Using Cleveland High School as a model, Principal Candace Stevens and her staff at Greenway Elementary in Beaverton, Oregon, developed their own philosophy statement directed more toward younger students. It is as follows:

> Greenway school is a learning environment in which all members of the community feel comfortable, involved, and challenged. We are responsible to each other for behavior that exhibits an awareness of respect for human dignity and individual differences. We share the responsibility of maintaining a safe climate that promotes and encourages learning.
>
> Greenway students have the right to equal educational opportunity and the right to know the rationale for the rules and decisions affecting them. They are in jeopardy of losing their rights when their individual actions infringe on the rights, needs, or property of others. If a rule is broken, a consequence will be applied that is commensurate and compatible with the infraction. Employing an educational model for solving discipline problems is in keeping with the learning environment.
>
> Our primary goal is to prepare students to be contributing members of a society which uses a democratic process. It is hoped that students who leave Greenway School will possess academic and social skills that will begin to prepare them to function as responsible citizens.

Because first impressions are so long remembered, school personnel should devote time and resources to carefully shape rules that are clear and concise, emphasize the behavior desired, and whenever possible, the reasons for the rules. Giving reasons for rules has the effect of trusting students to think for themselves as well as having the appearance that the rule is not arbitrary. For example, instead of "no street shoes on the gym floor," create a rule which elicits responsible decision making, such as, "Wear shoes which will not damage the gym floor." Clarify, describe, and teach the desired behavior and avoid the use of negative statements. "Move carefully in the halls," might replace "No running in the halls." The "do not" rules should be necessary only in case of potential danger or a compelling need for clarity.

⚖
Judicious Consequences

When a rule is broken, educators usually begin thinking in one of two directions: what punishment would expedite a cessation of the problem, or, which educational strategies and resources will be most effective in bringing about a "teachable moment." Each mindset conjures up various scenarios, at times mutually exclusive, which eventually will become the basis of new expectations as consequences are played out. If educators would direct their thoughts and efforts toward utilizing their professional preparation and educational expertise as the way to resolve problems, students would not perceive consequences as punishment, but as opportunities to learn acceptable behaviors and better attitudes with the enabling guidance of teachers and administrators dedicated to helping all students succeed.

Because an educator's first disciplinary move sets a definitive stamp on the school or classroom environment, an underlying philosophy for shaping consequences must be carefully weighed and practiced until, like second nature, it becomes a spontaneous approach to behavioral problems. Having fair and reasonable rules is important, but more often than not, good discipline is directly related to the way educators handle violations and exceptions to rules. Rules serve their purpose and are effective only until they are broken. When a rule is violated, the burden of maintaining classroom and school discipline shifts to a workable consequence. The consequence then becomes the rule. Because of this entanglement between rules and consequences, **judicious rules necessitate judicious consequences**.

There are two important aspects of judicious consequences. The first is a consequence which is commensurate with the rule violation, and the second is one compatible with the needs of the student and the school community. **Commensurate** denotes the consequence is consistent with and flows logically from the student's misbehavior. **Compatible** represents a broader view of the problem, and includes issues ranging from the students' need for personal self-worth and academic achievement, to the effect the students' behavior has on school and classroom environments. For example, a commensurate consequence might logically have a despoiling student scrub graffiti from the walls, but to be compatible with the student's educational and self-esteem needs, the work would be done after school and thus prevent missed class time and the ridicule of peers.

Commensurate, or logical, consequences are common to many classroom management strategies and provide a good beginning when determining a judicious consequence. But if logic is the only criteria, it may turn out to be ineffectual or even lead to other problems. Let's take the example of two students talking to each other during silent reading. One action which could be considered logical would be for the teacher to announce, "If you two feel it necessary to talk, then go right on talking. When you finish, the rest of us will be able to go back to our reading." This method of discipline is called satiation and appears from many teachers' viewpoint to be reasonably applied in this situation. However, not all students would perceive the teacher's statement as only a cue to stop talking but interpret the approach as demeaning and punishing. Too often students are more responsive to the teachers' conduct and choice of the consequence, than to the fact their behavior was detrimental to others. Because a commensurate consequence is designed only to flow from an infraction, it often obscures other important issues surrounding the event. It is imperative, therefore, to consider carefully the compatible aspect of judicious consequences before taking appropriate action.

The compatible nature of judicious consequences embodies an holistic approach and implies a resolution which balances all ramifications and possibilities. **Developing the compatible aspect begins with identifying issues central to the educational and self-esteem needs of students as well as to the mission and ethical practices of professional educators.** A few examples of professionally responsible questions are as follows:

    1. What needs to be learned here?

    2. How would an educator manage the problem?

    3. Do I need more information about the student or the student's family?

    4. What strategies can we use to keep this student in school?

    5. How will the student perceive the consequence?

    6. How will it affect the school community?

    7. **And**, in order for the important issues of the problem to unfold and for workable solutions to take form; how can I keep intact the mutual respect needed for a strong student/educator relationship throughout the life of the consequence?

Educators must examine all the relevant issues of a student's education if they are to develop a judicious style--a professional posture of having authority to decide and act, but not until the pivotal questions are realized and carefully weighed. If asked to retitle *Judicious Discipline*, I would call it something like *Who, What, When, Where, Why, and How to Back Off*. This is not to be confused with backing down or inaction, but simply an approach to seeing all sides of the question before being responsive to the problem. Sometimes instead of trying to be so inventive or manipulative, educators should allow natural forces to bring about a resolution or let what happens play itself out. Too often needless panic or exaggeration of the problem exacerbates the situation and an "us against them" mentality pervades. Educators must work to instill a certain confidence in students and parents that the school community is in the capable hands of concerned and conscientious professionals. A hammer or a chisel can be very useful tools for resolving some building problems, but other jobs require the delicate manipulation of tiny Phillips screwdrivers or needle-nosed pliers. The analogy fits the educator who does not try to use a hammer to solve every problem, but carries a tool box filled with strategies and ideas for the purpose of building students' knowledge and self-esteem. Fair and reasonable rules are without question important but, more often than not, the styling of the consequence is decisive in the resolution of the problem. An educator with workable ideas is an educator with patience and self-assurance.

In determining a judicious consequence for each student, it is important to understand the real nature of the problem as well as account for the **individual differences among students**. For example, if two culpable students were asked to clean a vandalized wall and one student replies, "I have the time right after school," and the other belligerently responds, "That's not my job, that's janitor's work," different consequences should be played out for each student. In the case of the first student, the wall would be cleaned willingly, and in all likelihood this would not be perceived as punishment but rather as an act of restitution from a responsible student making amends for a mistake. As for the other student, scrubbing the wall becomes secondary to the defiant attitude now apparent as the underlying problem. Educational resources and effective communication become necessary as a means of understanding the reason for the student's attitude and successfully resolving the student's problem. As the true

nature of the difficulty presents itself and workable resolutions
emerge, judicious consequences directly related to that student's
individual needs are developed and carried out. Although the
second student may not clean the wall in question, a subsequent
change of attitude could result in the student choosing to rectify
his past indiscretions by participating in other cleanup activities.
On the other hand, if both students feel forced to clean the wall,
the first student would resent the punishment and its demeaning
nature and the second student's problems would not only go
unnoticed and unattended, but could encourage retaliation and
an escalation of damage to school property.

One of the problems educators often express when considering individualizing consequences is the fear that students will
fault them as being unfair if others are treated differently. Those
employing punishment models are forced to be consistent, as
students are usually quick to remind educators their punishment
was not the same as that which others received for the same
offense. On the other hand, judicious consequences by definition
respect individual differences among students and allow more
flexibility by styling consequences to meet the educational and
self-esteem needs of all parties involved. When students perceive
consequences as educational in nature, feel they make sense for
them and are acting on their own volition, they should show little
interest in comparing their situation to that of others. The variety
of educational methods educators employ to remedy individual
learning problems are seldom questioned by students. Why,
therefore, should students object to educators employing different consequences as they work with the many different
individual needs and attitudes their fellow students bring to
behavioral problems?

Consequences originally designed to punish can easily be
altered to emphasize the educational needs of students. For
example, students who skip school frequently often have the
feeling school authorities are more concerned with punishing
students for breaking the rules than helping them make up
missed school work or with resolving other problems that give

rise to absences, such as a parent who wants them at home. At a recent workshop I conducted, I was confronted by a school superintendent who said, "What could be more logical than to require students who skip school, to attend Saturday school to make up the school work missed?" I replied that he had just given us an example of a punishment model for skipping school. A judicious model, I explained, would inform students that the school is open Saturday and staffed with tutors willing to help them make up the work missed in order to be prepared to return to class on Monday morning. Both models constitute Saturday school, but one is perceived by the student as punishment and the other as an opportunity, with special help from the system, to learn and succeed in school. The consequence for missing class then becomes an educational consequence of school work that must be made up during the student's own time. Unlike consequences that punish students, judicious consequences are not as easily construed by students as contrived or unfair.

A cooperative approach would be to solicit consequences from the student or ask a student to choose among several possibilities: a parent conference, a talk with the school counselor, performing a public service project, or even time for themselves away from the school. All of these possibilities can be effective as long as both commensurate and compatible issues are carefully and thoughtfully weighed before determining and administering student consequences.

Educators should avoid voicing or publishing specific consequences before behavioral problems occur. Teachers and administrators who play their hand prior to the problem often box themselves into a poor decision that, when examined in the light of extenuating circumstances, could have been resolved through use of a more appropriate and instructive consequence. Another problem with predetermined consequences is that students often play games with the rules and consequences. For example, knowing that the third infraction means being sent to the office almost invites two disruptions by an irresponsible student. When narrow lines are drawn, students seem to want to stand on them.

But educators who draw broad lines students must walk across will enjoy better rapport and improved discipline as they allow themselves options and time to work out individual problems.

Class discussion of possible consequences is an important aspect of student due process rights. Students have a right to know what they can expect from minor to major infringements of the rules. If students are involved in formulating consequences appropriate to the rule violations, they will not only understand the supporting rationale and feel a shared ownership, but are more likely to accept the consequences when administered. Just as students are taught the reasons for the rules, they need to know and discuss the reasons supporting the consequences of their actions. The time and effort spent on the commensurate and compatible aspect of judicious consequences will provide the give-and-take needed to establish confidence in the teacher's professional ability and the resolve to pursue student indiscretions. How students perceive educator's intentions is directly related to the judicious manner in which consequences are shaped, conveyed, and put into practice.

I have often wondered why some students enjoy discovering what they can get away with in certain classes, but in other classes behave in an entirely different manner. I have come to the conclusion that students find no fun at all trying to disrupt a class in which they perceive the teacher is trying to help them succeed in school and really cares about their future. Many argue, however, that judicious consequences are not tough enough and will not deter students from misbehavior. In the short run there is some validity to these arguments, but if attitudes about the importance of learning and succeeding in school are to be encouraged and exemplified, we must opt for strategies which will be effective over the long haul.

Educators who develop a judicious approach to consequences will earn a level of student trust and respect which in the course of time allows them to transcend the need for establishing consequences for every student misbehavior. If students know that consequences for their misconduct will be judicious in nature, as opposed to punishing, then consequences become akin to a curriculum issue and not a matter of depriving one of liberty or property rights. When students believe they are in the capable hands of a professional educator, judicious consequences are perceived by students as educational activities designed to help them overcome their behavior problems. When this plateau of mutual trust and professional responsibility has been achieved, good educational and ethical practice become the model for student discipline.

The First Day of Classes

Good classroom discipline begins with an educator's belief that all students have value and are capable of proper social interaction. While it is important to establish the boundaries necessary for a positive educational atmosphere, it is equally important to communicate to students the fact they are an integral part of school operations and that they and their opinions are worthy. Often student handbooks or classroom rules convey the impression that rules are chiseled in stone with little or no student involvement. Ironically, it is not the rules that keep students in school and behaving appropriately, it is the philosophy and attitude with which the educator approaches rules and consequences that convinces students they belong in school.

Though it is preferable to devote adequate class time to rules and consequences, the logistics and practicality may vary greatly from one classroom to another. Self-contained classrooms where students are together most of the day, all year long, present greater opportunities for student input and discussion than classes which meet once a day in 40- or 50-minute sessions for part of the school year. Although strategies may differ, the goal of shared ownership for classroom rules remains the same.

▬▬▬*Inductive Approach*

In a self-contained classroom, for example, teachers have the opportunity to employ an **inductive approach** to classroom rules and consequences. Two associates, Dr. Barbara McEwan, an assistant professor of education at the State University of New York campus at Cortland, and Margaret Abbott, a fourth grade teacher in the West Linn, Oregon, school district, have been field testing *Judicious Discipline* and offer the following as an example of a lesson plan for fourth graders using the inductive approach:

**Understanding Rights and Creating Rules
in a Democratic Classroom**

Objective: To inform students of their rights and when they lose their rights according to society's needs. To provide students with an opportunity to apply that information to the development of classroom rules.

Opening: "Take out a piece of paper and pencil. As fast as you can, write down all the individual rights you think you have in our country." (Put their responses on the board.)

"Now, write down all the rights you think you have when you're in school." (Put these responses on the board.)

"Would you be surprised to find out that your rights as citizens of our country and your rights in school are almost the same?

"Today we will be discussing the citizenship rights you have in a public school classroom and when you can lose those rights.

"Understanding the rights we all have and knowing what actions can cause us to lose those rights helps us to become responsible citizens in school and in our society."

Procedure: Say to the students, "Let's look again at the rights we've put on the board. Let's see if there is a way to group them into categories. First, how do we know we have these rights? Who or what tells us that we do?"

Guide students through a brief review of the *Constitution*

and Amendments.

"In school you have all your rights protected. You even have more rights in a classroom than I do." (Use example of students wearing political buttons, but teachers refraining from such a statement.)

"For the most part there are three amendments that are very important to remember in school: The First, Fourth, and Fourteenth." Follow with a brief explanation of what these amendments include.

"Who can tell me which of the rights on the board would come from the 1st Amendment? The Fourth? The Fourteenth?" (Teacher should fill in the gaps as needed.)

"You are citizens in my classroom and I will treat you accordingly.

"I am a citizen in this town, state, and country. When I'm not in this classroom, I am entitled to all of my rights. What does that mean? Does that mean I can do anything I want to? Can I do anything I feel like doing?" Brainstorm and list on the board actions the teacher cannot do outside of the classroom.

"When we put your rights on the board we were able to group them into different amendments. Let's look at your ideas about when I lose my rights and see if we can discover some headings those actions would fit under. In your groups of four, work together to see if you can find headings or categories for the situations on the board."

In five minutes check to see if they have discovered any patterns to the actions. Put up their ideas for categories and display a poster of the four compelling state interests. Briefly explain them.

"When society takes away my rights, they do it because of a compelling state interest. I can't throw a rock through a store window or run a red light or yell fire in a theatre. As citizens in this classroom, you will lose your rights if I can show a compelling state interest applies to something you are doing. Let's look again at the compelling state interests. In your groups, take a few minutes to discuss what actions students might engage in that

would result in them losing their rights because of a compelling
state interest."

In five minutes bring groups back together to share their
ideas.

"Now that you have an understanding of what rights you
have and when you can lose those rights, let's think together how
we can use this information to develop rules for our class. What
rules could we develop that would match each one of the compelling state interests? What would be a reasonable classroom
rule to reflect property loss and damage?" Work through each of
the compelling state interests.

Closing: "Now that we have discussed your citizenship rights
and developed classroom rules based on the compelling state
interests, we are ready for the next step.

"Tomorrow we will talk about judicious consequences. You
will learn what they are and help to create consequences for our
classroom that are fair and make sense."

Margie Abbott had been teaching fifteen years before she
began to use the concepts of *Judicious Discipline* in her classroom. She had always started the year by asking her students
what rules they think they need for their class. Many different
rules were suggested, but she always felt a need for an organizer
to bring them all together. Margie found that by teaching her
students about their constitutional rights and how the compelling
state interests take away those rights, her class not only had a
legal framework for their rules but also learned the rationale our
government uses as the basis of our nation's morality.

The wording for the rules came from the students after each
compelling state interest was explained and understood. Time
was spent discussing the intent of the rules, the significance of
each, and the concerns students expressed. Questions were
encouraged to eliminate uncertainty. When the rules were clearly
understood, they were posted in the classroom. Each student
then signed the rules poster, agreeing to follow them to the best
of their ability. This year Margie's class agreed to the following

rules based on the four compelling state interests:

1. Respect other people's property.
2. We are here to listen and learn.
3. Conduct yourself in a safe manner and be healthy.
4. Be yourself. Do not seriously disrupt the class.

Deductive Approach

On the other hand, educators meeting five or six classes a day for 40 to 50 minutes each are not only under time constraints, but need consistent sets of classroom rules. These teachers are more likely to employ a **deductive approach** to establishing classroom rules. The following are some ideas for secondary teachers:

1. Briefly review the history of the change from school rules based on the concept of *in loco parentis* to today's need to consider student civil rights when developing rules and consequences (see page 15).

2. Talk about how you will approach rules and consequences (see pages 28-40). A possible scenario might be as follows:

"I believe it is my professional responsibility not only to recognize and respect your rights as a citizen in this classroom, but to help you live within those rights. Balancing your human rights with society's need for an effective educational environment will form the basis for my classroom rules and decisions. When it comes to weighing the consequences for rule infractions, I will strive to keep them commensurate with your actions and compatible with your need for personal self-worth and educational opportunities (use example on page 30 about the student who defaces property or one you have used previously in class). I feel it is my responsibility to teach you your citizenship rights in school and how you lose your rights as well as the demeanor and know-how necessary for all of us to benefit from a good educational experience. If the time comes when you lose your rights,

I will make every effort to be evenhanded as we work through the problem together. Rules and decisions in this class will simply be for helping you succeed as a student."

3. Explain that the First, Fourth, and Fourteenth Amendments are those most often applied to student rights (see page 8) and how the four compelling state interests come into play to take away those rights (see page 18). Use examples from your class or others such as:

> a. Student speech and how it applies to the school dress code (see page 83).
>
> b. Students' free exercise of religion and the schools' responsibility not to establish religion (see page 96).
>
> c. Student press and the distribution or posting of opinions (see page 92).
>
> d. Student searches and the need for reasonable suspicion by school authorities (see page 87).
>
> e. The equal protection clause and a student's right to an equal educational opportunity in addition to fair and equal treatment under school rules and decisions (see page 10).
>
> f. Due process and a student's right to fair and legal rules, notice, a hearing, and an appeal (see page 10).

By using examples of how our justice system weighs the requisites of managing an effective educational environment against a person's individual rights, students should be able to understand that their rights are not a license to do as they please in school.

4. Set forth your ideals about how you view the responsibilities and ethics of professional educators. Some topic ideas to be elaborated upon might be as follows:

> a. Student-centered: "I recognize that each of you bring different educational and personal needs to this classroom. My goal is to address your individual needs as often as I am able in

an effort to help each of you enjoy learning and achieve success in school this year." (see page 121).

b. Student/educator relationship: "We have a student/teacher relationship similar to a doctor/patient and lawyer/client relationship. It is very important to me that we continue this association through good times as well as when problems may develop between us."

c. Positive educational practices: "I would like you to know how I feel about teaching and discipline and where I plan to direct my energies and priorities." (see page 122).

d. List of **Nevers**: "Let's talk about what experience has taught me and some things I never want to do again." (see page 125).

e. Student ethics: "Now that we have discussed my professional ethics, let's consider the ethics of being a good student, i.e. honesty, promptness, consideration of others, etc." (see page 130).

Note: If the history of student rights and applicable amendments are already covered by the student handbook and/or other teachers, educators may want to recognize these concepts only in passing and devote more time to their application in their classroom.

Encourage questions and discussion about the interpretation and meaning of the rules and regulations. Sometimes an open discussion of rules and behavior will prevent feelings of being ignored and create a sense of responsibility for the adopted classroom policies. By involving the students in a dialogue of reasons for our country's rules, the teacher is not only teaching citizenship and critical thinking skills, but has brought about a sense of awareness for upholding the individual rights of others. Show students a copy of *Judicious Discipline* and encourage them to read it. If students know it will be the basis for your decisions

affecting their property and liberty interests, many may feel
motivated to check it out. The return on this investment of time
and effort is a student's proprietary interest in school and a
feeling of accountability for rules and consequences.

Although most secondary teachers use the deductive approach, Bill Howry, an English teacher at Corvallis High School
in Corvallis, Oregon, found the inductive process worked very
well for him. The following is his narrative of how he begins his
classes:

"After teaching high school students for nineteen years, I
have just completed my most successful year in the business. In
the middle of June, my students and I are still enjoying a mutual
respect, and most of us feel that the year has been not only
enjoyable, but worthwhile. A large part of this success stems
from a two-week unit I conducted in mid-September.

"Following a few days of diagnostic testing, I opened the
class one day with a proposal that since we were in this together
and for the duration, perhaps we needed some guidelines to
coexist by. Freshmen are fairly used to rules being imposed on
them, and, being new to the high school system, they were
willing to listen to any I had concocted for them. Instead, I asked
them to come up with their own set of rules. This excited some
and worried others. I asked them to work in small groups to
compose the ten most necessary guidelines to live by in our
classroom.

"Surprisingly enough, all groups seriously attacked the
assignment. After fifteen groups (from all three of my Freshman
English classes) had turned in their lists, I compiled a composite
list to hand back to them. Here are the top ten, including the
number of times each rule appeared on any list:

    1. Do not distract others from their work. (6)
    2. Chewing gum is allowed. (4)
    3. Students may discuss assignments with each
    other. (4)
    4. Respect the teacher and your classmates. (4)

5. Students may write notes or do other homework if finished with the day's assignments. (3)
6. Do not talk in a loud, disruptive manner. (3)
7. Do not talk while the teacher is talking. (3)
8. Students are allowed to leave class for a good
reason. (2)
9. Always bring study materials (books, pencil,
paper) to class. (2)
10. Raise your hand before speaking. (2)

"Other rules that appeared on lists included keeping one's hands to oneself, being able to wear hats and sunglasses, not running in the classroom, and being assured that the teacher would not confront a student in front of the class. When I handed the composite list back to them (twenty-five rules in all), no one seemed too surprised at the absolute tone or the large number of rules.

"I then asked them to lay the list aside for a few days and to take notes on what I was about to tell them. Being new to both me and the system, they were amenable to this, too.

"The next few days were spent in discussion (using an overhead projector to emphasize certain words and concepts) of the principles of *Judicious Discipline.* I began with the concept of balance: the rights of the majority and the freedoms of individuals. I discussed the basic values of freedom, justice and equality. We overviewed the First, Fourth and Fourteenth Amendments, focusing on the Fourteenth. I gave them a new term and, for many, a new concept: compelling state interest. We covered each state interest, discussing examples for each. I provided them with some landmark cases; they came up with some interesting hypothetical cases of their own.

"Finally, being fairly sure that they understood the concept of compelling state interest, I asked them to take out their list of rules for a second look. We proceeded through the list, evaluating each rule against the compelling state interest categories. Students were quick to see whether each of their rules was compatible with the concept of compelling state interest.

"Immediately following this discussion, I gave them an outline of guidelines I consider fair. Since the guidelines I suggested were based on what we had just spent four days talking about, there was practically no discussion. I suspected that they were willing to give the system a try.

"Now, in June, I feel that they actually did try. I followed through with the policies of due process in grading and behavior matters. I kept an open gradebook and an open mind. I confronted students occasionally, but not in front of their peers. While other factors may have contributed to the cause, I am sure of the effect. I had fewer tardies and other discipline problems than I have had in the past ten years. I had few problems with late papers. I was delighted much more often than I was disappointed. And I have seen the students reach goals I really didn't think possible at the beginning of the year."

Occasionally teachers believe they are creating a democratic environment when they seek a consensus from the class or allow students to vote on an issue. This is not always a good idea nor does it accurately reflect our democratic way of life. For example, a class may want to decide by majority vote that an orthopedically-impaired student should be excluded from field trips because it would slow down the group, or that a pregnant girl may not run for a student body office. Students should be helped to understand that if the matter involves student rights, the question is simply not open to majority vote. Our democratic form of government only allows us to vote on those issues which are not protected by the *Constitution*. There are occasions, especially in the area of student privileges, when majority votes are appropriate and should be encouraged. For example, there should be no problem allowing students to decide which band will play at the dance, or whether to serve ice cream or popcorn at the class party, etc.

For visual purposes, I have developed a chart and some ideas for school and classroom rules based on the four compelling state interests and applicable judicious consequences. My purpose is to present these concepts together in outline form to illustrate how they might be organized when presented to students. These examples are not meant to be all inclusive, but to serve as illustrations of the possibilities that can be adapted to various teaching and administrative styles.

The advantage of teaching and administering rules founded on our nation's laws is that teachers and administrators do not personally identify with the rules. When personal biases are used as the basis for school rules, school authorities are likely to become personally involved, thereby causing an escalation of a personality conflict which has no relevance to the student's education. A constitutional perspective allows teachers and administrators to remain objective, analogous to a third party whose role it is to shepherd the relationship between the student and the rules. The fruits of this labor are clearly felt when calmly responding to an inquiring or quarrelsome student, "If you don't like these rules, you may be surprised by the rules into which you will be graduating." Two hundred plus years of integrated wisdom and authority properly presented and discussed can work wonders for teachers and administrators seeking to bring about a school year of mutual regard and respect.

⚖️

Outline for Formulating

Rules and Consequences

Property Loss and Damage

Rules: Rules should cover both school and personal property. Writing and discussing these rules offers a good opportunity to teach students respect for the property of others as well as ways to be responsible for and take care of personal property brought to school.

Examples of Consequences: Could include:
> apology
> clean it up
> give it back
> restitution
> mutual agreements
> community service project
> counseling
> conference with parents
> reassignment
> loss of privileges
> suspension
> expulsion

Legitimate Educational Purpose

Rules: These are rules and decisions made by lawmakers and professional educators about educational content and process. It is difficult to include student input but important to discuss with students and parents the educational rationale behind the rules that direct their educational standards and requirements.

Examples of Consequences: Could include:
> apology
> redo the assignment or take another test
> complete an alternate assignment
> study with a tutor
> a private conference
> mutual agreement
> counseling
> conference with parents
> reassignment
> loss of privileges
> suspension
> expulsion

Health and Safety

Rules: Rules should be drafted to protect both the individual student as well as the others in the group. A good discussion topic for students to learn to appreciate a central role of government.

Examples of Consequences: Could include:
> apology
> complete a research report
> community service project
> a private conference
> mutual agreements
> counseling
> conference with parents
> reassignment
> loss of privileges
> suspension
> expulsion

Serious Disruption of the Educational Process

Rules: Rules should reflect the importance of maintaining a positive learning environment and emphasize responsible behavior to self and others seeking to learn. Discuss the importance of being able to handle minor distractions which would allow others to exercise certain individual rights, who should the rule be directed against, and whether or not there is a legitimate need for the rule. This state interest provides excellent material on student rights issues and offers a good opportunity to develop critical thinking skills.

Examples of Consequences: Could include:
> apology
> a private conference

mutual agreements
time out
problem solving room
counseling
mediation
conference with parents
reassignment
community service
loss of privileges
suspension
expulsion

Part III

The Balance: Synthesis and Evaluation

The Balance is the synthesis and evaluation of student constitutional rights, good educational practice, and professional ethics counterbalanced with the problems and practical realities of student discipline and achievement. Although some of the subject matter examined in Part III may appear to have little to do with discipline, the subtle nature of discriminatory practices cuts deep into students' feelings of self-worth and is often the cause for putting students "at risk." For instance, how many times does a teacher have to repeat jokes demeaning a student's ethnic heritage before the student loses interest in school or begins a pattern of disruptive behavior? Often it is a risky educational environment which spawns and serves as the lifeblood of "at risk" students.

Whereas Part I presents a framework which is well established and has served our nation for two hundred years, Part III is constantly changing. The dynamics of The Balance require educators to stay abreast of new laws and educational practice in an effort to meet society's increasing demands on public schools. As we search for ways to create an environment which provides an equal educational opportunity for all students, keep in mind the scales of justice with one student looking across at all the other students. We must not only consider the demands of the majority, but also remain conscious of individual needs and desires. The Balance provides educators a sensible, consistent, and judicious rationale for rules and decisions affecting student achievement and behavior.

⚖️

Compulsory School Attendance

Attendance policies serve as societies' gates to educational opportunities or function as the walls of discouragement and despair for the student at risk. Legislation and the threat of expulsion simply do not insure good attendance. Many schools attempt to intimidate students by beginning their attendance policies with a statement of the state law followed by a long list of consequences. To many students this is perceived as a threat that "you better come to school or we will kick you out." As uninviting and incongruent as these rules are, their primary purpose is to keep desirables in and undesirables out, often resulting in a push-out phenomenon. In order to create the feeling of a helpful and safe environment where students want to be and feel they will be able to achieve success, a more appealing and professionally responsible approach must be taken.

Developing an effective attendance policy begins by educators asking themselves who it is they are responsible to teach and serve. Is it, for example, educators' responsibility to teach and serve students who skip classes, those with behavior problems, academic deficiencies, bad attitudes, or whose cultural values are offensive? If, in fact, building faculty and administration agree to provide an equal educational opportunity to all who come through the schoolhouse doors, the answer to these and other similar questions is yes. The gate will be open and a commitment to help all students will be mirrored in the attendance policy. If the answer is no, the walls will be put in place to bar these and others seen as less worthy from the benefits of public schooling. Because of the importance of this predisposition, educators must carefully examine their professional mission as they decide their standard of educational responsibility. Good student attendance is founded upon an "attendance philosophy" mutually shared by students and faculty. An excellent example of educational responsibility is the statement by the Cleveland High School faculty and administration previously described on page 38.

As necessary as our compulsory attendance laws are to establish expectations for students, they are often the cause of antithetical situations for educators to resolve. Most school districts are governed by state laws which mandate a specific number of **days required** to attend high school in order to graduate. However, when strictly enforced, the attendance requirement may not appear to be reasonably connected to its original intent. For example, a high school senior with a combined SAT score of 1250 and absent more than the permissible number of days, has a good argument that the attendance requirement should not prevent graduation. The question is whether to allow the student to graduate or require the student to return the following fall term to make up for seat-time missed. Although graduating a non-attending student may violate the letter of the law, a 1250 SAT score suggests the student has met the spirit of the laws' intent. Although not flawless, rules pertaining to the number of school days required for graduation should be used as guidelines, but their enforcement should be based on the facts relevant to each individual case.

Another issue related to attendance is **credit denial** and **dropping students** after a specified number of absences. This rule has value for the smooth administration of a school and legally must include an appeal process for students who wish to return during the same grading period. At question is not the validity of the rule or the appeal process, but rather the individual circumstances which serve as the substance of the appeal. Administrators need to consider each individual case carefully and base decisions on whether or not the student is able to complete the course work satisfactorily. If students can show an ability to complete the work adequately without causing an undue hardship for the teacher, permission should be granted to complete the required work regardless of the motive behind the absences. Those students who cannot finish the required work could be assigned to alternative education classes for the remainder of the grading period, where tutoring and individualized instruction would be available. Too often a student's reasons for extended absences will lead administrators into a quagmire of family values or personal freedoms, and therefore should not be made the basis for the student's return. Decide the issue of readmission based on sound educational practices and avoid moral judgments. The purpose of attendance is to facilitate learning. If students can demonstrate they are learning or have acquired "an education" by other means, they should not be denied the opportunity for an education or its subsequent benefits as punishment for nonattendance.

Another common problem is the quandary over **excused and unexcused absences**. Take, for instance, two students who skip school all day to play video games together at a local convenience store. One parent is willing to write an excused absence and the other parent is not. Although they were together during the absence, the students may experience very different consequences when they return to school. The excused student is usually given reasonable help to complete the school work missed and the other will probably be punished with a short suspension as well as not being allowed to make up missed tests and assignments. Three contradictory questions come to mind: Should we remove from the school and relinquish to parents the decision for excused and unexcused absences? If attendance is important to learning, why do we further exacerbate the problem with more missed class time? And, why is a student being punished with absence, exactly what the rules forbid? Administrators can avoid these antithetical situations by not distinguishing between excused and unexcused absences and only record student absences. If a student without a prearranged absence is not in attendance, contact could be made with a parent or guardian informing them of this fact. Hold parents and guardians accountable for their child's school attendance and treat the problem as an academic matter. Students excused to decorate for a carnival or who participate in sports often miss as much class time as wayfaring skippers. It makes it easier for educators to live with their inconsistencies if the consequence of being absent, for any reason, is to make up the school work missed.

Every educator knows when students miss class they lose the benefits of learning that occur in the normal course of classroom activities. To compensate for lost classroom learning, **educational alternatives** could be developed and required that are closely related to the classroom discussions and activities missed during students' absences. Examples of educational alternatives for absent students could be a term paper covering the subject matter discussed, a book review on the subject, or several pages outlining the missed chapters. To alleviate the overload generated by educational alternatives and make-up work, schools could provide tutors and schedule times during the school day, evenings, or week-ends when help would be available. The school could extend library hours for students as well as encourage parents and other family members to become involved. Well-planned alternative assignments not only offer students their right to equal opportunities, but recognize individual differences in learning styles and emphasize the importance of class rigor and academic expectations. In the event that alternative assignments are viewed by some students as punishment for being absent, a straightforward and understandable explanation would be necessary to illustrate that it is an educational expectation in lieu of what students learned in class. I was confronted at a recent workshop by a teacher who asked, "Are you telling me that if a student has been ill and another was skipping, that they should both be able to make up the work missed?" My response was that both needed an educator when they returned, perhaps the one who skipped more than the other. Regardless of the reason for the students' absences, make up work and late assignments should be accepted to insure those students an **equal educational opportunity**.

Tardiness is difficult to manage with any degree of consistency because of problems associated with its definition. In an effort to be consistent, many schools employ strict rules and a punishment approach to alleviate the problem. A typical rule in most schools has tardy students sent to the office for an excuse, after three unexcused tardies they report for detention, and after the next three tardies are suspended for a day or two. This punishment approach often leads to other educational and administrative problems, such as time allocated to students obtaining excuses, class disruption for a second time, students playing games with the rule by unnecessarily being late twice but not the critical third time, difficulty in judging or proving excuses, and finally learning more about following rules than becoming responsible for their own behavior.

Rules and consequences for tardiness should attempt to mitigate educational disruptions as well as teach and encourage the value of being on time. For this reason, teachers are in the best position to regulate tardiness, and should be given the authority to resolve their own problems. The first day of class could begin by discussing with students how to enter the classroom late, thereby alleviating the disturbance associated with tardiness. Ask students who are tardy to remain after class to discuss the reasons. If the reasons make sense the matter is closed. If not, work on a mutually agreeable plan in an effort to arrive at a reasonable solution. If the problem is one of attitude, focus efforts on changing the student's feelings about the importance of punctuality. If necessary, recruit the help of counselors or other educators who have good rapport with the student.

One of the best strategies to discourage tardiness is for

teachers to start class on time. A well-prepared, ready-to-go teacher, modeling behavior congruent with expectations sends a powerful message to a lingering student. Approaching tardiness as an educator will go further to alleviate the problem than if it is viewed as a game or foul play in need of punishment. Administrators should become involved only with chronic problems or when teachers have exhausted their own resources in attempting to solve the problem.

Suspension is a short-term denial of the student's right to the benefits of public education. This may range from very short in-house suspensions to removal from school for a period up to seven to thirty days, depending on state laws. Because the absence is usually brief, a student suffers no substantial loss of educational opportunities. For this reason the law accords students mostly procedural due process rights. These procedural rights were set out in *Goss v. Lopez*, 419 U.S. 565, and require the administrator to provide at least:

> 1. Notice--an oral or written notice of the charges; i.e., the rule the student violated.
> 2. Evidence--a summary of the evidence against the student; i.e., a teacher witnessed the student's misbehavior.
> 3. Defense--an opportunity for the student to be heard; i.e., the student has an opportunity to tell his or her side of the story.

If the student demands an attorney or presentation of witnesses, an administrator may choose not to comply with the student's demands unless local law holds otherwise. The court balanced a student's right to procedural due process against the school's need not to be overburdened with time-consuming student hearings.

Although courts have dealt only with suspensions from school, fair and consistent building policy would require the same three steps be taken by teachers who consider the removal of a student from the classroom. On most occasions, if a teacher would take the time to explain the problem and hear the student's side of a story, a better decision than having the student leave the classroom might be made.

Administrative style is crucial to a judicious suspension and often pivotal to influencing the student's attitude when he or she returns to school. For example, suspension could be meted out as punishment ("this will teach you a lesson") or as a chance to get away from school and cool down a bit ("we could both use time away from each other"). The second implies that considerable effort was made to help the student, but a resolution of the problem could not been reached. When students must be suspended, communicate the school's interest in their welfare by providing them with academic assignments and offering them after school and week-end tutoring. Walk the student to the bicycle rack or to the parking lot. Call them during their suspension to wish them well and to say that you are looking forward to their return. Being excluded from the school community is painful and educators who remain friends do much to alleviate the loneliness and bitterness associated with the separation. Essential to a judicious suspension is an administrative style sensitive to the self-esteem needs of the student: a style that fosters and supports a positive attitude toward school and keeps intact the all-important student/educator relationship.

Expulsions are for a longer duration than suspensions and usually result in the loss of grades and credits, and the result is a substantial deprivation of educational opportunity. For this reason, students faced with such a consequence have both substantive and procedural due process rights. Not only must schools provide the charges, evidence, and a hearing, but must also substantiate the reasons for expulsion. In addition, students have a right to be represented by counsel, review all records, bring witnesses, cross examine, receive a complete and accurate record of the proceedings, and appeal the decision. As with suspensions, every effort should be made to communicate the school's interest in the students' welfare, including advice and help in locating alternative educational opportunities.

Handicapped students have additional rights that do not

flow to non-handicapped students. Because a handicapping condition may be cause for a suspension or expulsion, federal and state laws require other procedures which must be followed. To stay informed of the changing law in the field of special education, administrators should seek advice from special educators and legal counsel in matters pertaining to both suspensions and expulsions of handicapped students.

⚖️
Grading Practices

Grades are generally perceived by society as a summation of academic achievement. However, due to the excessive entanglement between **achievement** and **behavior**, achievement grades are often misapplied and as a result, become misleading. The use of grade reduction or augmentation has become all too commonplace in an effort to find a cure-all to control student behavior. Grade reduction for unexcused absences, insolence, missing a concert in music, not dressing down in physical education, and late papers are only a few examples of student behaviors affecting achievement grades. The ethical and legal problems inherent in these attempts to deter undesirable behavior through achievement records evidences itself in the misinformation passed on to others about the student's mastery of the subject.

An academically gifted student whose grade is lowered because of an occasional unexcused absence or demonstrated bad attitude is likely to be deprived of future opportunities. Misrepresenting student achievement affects students' Fourteenth Amendment **liberty** interests when this information is used by others to decide opportunities for scholarships, admission to classes or college, and job prospects. The letter grade on a report card or transcript is perceived as the student's level of skill and understanding of a subject matter. Those reading these grades are not privy to information accurately detailing the fact that the grade reflects an entanglement of behavior and achievement standards. The issue is not whether the grade belongs to the teacher or the student, but whether it communicates to the reader an accurate statement of the student's achievement. Although behavioral information is very important to those evaluating students, it should be passed on through verbal and written statements.

Notwithstanding the authority teachers have to determine curriculum and standards for grades, a student's liberty does not hinge on what the teacher thinks the grade means, but what the widespread consensus of those who interpret the grade think it means. For example, lowering a grade for a late assignment in a writing course would be different from lowering a grade for missing a deadline in a journalism class. Whereas learning punctuality in order to meet press time could be an expected achievement in a journalism class, it would not be considered achievement in a writing class. It is important to know and incorporate only those requirements and standards for grading which are commonly understood to be achieved within the course title. A plausible test would be to ask employers and college admissions personnel what they believe an "A" or a "C" means in classes titled "Advanced Welding" or "Algebra I."

I am reminded of a former student who returned to visit with me several years after completing one of my educational law courses. As an experienced English teacher she had always reasoned that with many papers to grade, a strategy was needed to pressure students to complete their work on time; the alternative she always feared was a deluge of papers at the end of the grading period. Lowering grades on late papers had been a satisfactory solution prior to taking my class; however, on examining the issue in light of students' liberty, she had felt unsure. After trying several alternatives that did not work, she finally settled on the following plan.

At the beginning of each new term she begins her class with a review of the course requirements, one of which is a short composition due every two weeks. She continues with an explanation that these assignments will be graded and returned within a few days. She expands on the educational value of writing practice, learning from mistakes, and the benefits of her written remarks and suggestions. In addition, the class is informed that she has over 150 students a week and has budgeted enough time to correct and return papers handed in on schedule. She emphasizes that it is to their educational advantage and her administrative convenience for compositions to be submitted on a regular basis. Next, she points to two boxes on her desk: one labeled "papers on time" and the other "late papers." She informs her students that papers coming in on time will be corrected and returned promptly as promised; late compositions will be graded and returned as time allows or sometime next semester. Students can expect an "Incomplete" on their report cards until the papers are corrected and the grades can be changed. In other words, late papers...late grades. She smiled and told me she now has no problem with late papers. No longer does she constantly have to remind students of deadlines; parents ceased to complain about unfair grades; and her students are accepting the responsibility for turning in their work on time.

Other teachers who have used this approach feel good about the fact that students are more likely to complete their late work if they know it will not be graded down, thereby learning and benefiting more from the class. Accepting late papers also communicates to students that all school work is important and that learning the subject matter or skills is more important than administrative convenience or just being able to meet a deadline. There are those who argue that accepting late work is unfair to other students because more time is allowed to complete the assignment. However, if all students are allowed the same prerogative, then all will have an equal opportunity to give the assignment their best effort. Teachers' fear of students "taking advantage" of the opportunity to complete late assignments keep many educators from placing so much responsibility in the hands of their students. Almost all who try this, however, discover their

fears to be unfounded and experience a sense of professional
pride in the fact their students are now doing their assignments
without all the prodding and loss of interest associated with late
work penalties. There is something antithetical about an educational assignment which is not accepted by an "educator" because it is late. The message this sends to students is that being
on time is **more** important than the educational value of the
coursework assigned. While this particular solution may not work
for every teacher, it is an illustration of placing responsibility on
the student as well as recording grades which reflect only academic achievement.

Educators often cite "real world" reasons to lower grades
for such things as tardiness, poor attitude, or late papers. They
argue these and other similar behavior patterns often lead to
being fired from jobs, and that teaching students this lesson will
prove beneficial later in life. This argument begins to unravel,
however, as employers have learned that employees' productivity
and attendance is not related as much to fear of dismissal as it
is to the positive aspects of personal accomplishment and pride
in the product or service. Employers have discovered it is not
good business to fire someone they have spent time and money
to hire and train only to have to go through the process again.
The trend in business and manufacturing today is to help work-
ers who are experiencing problems in the workplace succeed in
their job, offering assistance such as counseling, rehabilitation,
and retraining. If this approach is producing more and better
widgets, then the concepts of *Judicious Discipline* are as much a
model of the "real world" of business as of our nation's government.

Schools that allow and encourage teachers the judicious use
of an **Incomplete grade** offer their faculty many more opportunities to be creative and fair in their grading practices. This
option does not have the effect of diminishing class rigor or
expectations, and sends a message to students that until all
assignments and tests are complete and submitted, they will not
receive a grade or credit for the class. Prudent administrative

policy would allow a reasonable time for students to make up required work. This "reasonable time" could vary depending on the student's need for course credit or the availability of the teacher involved. If course work is not completed within this time frame, the "I" should remain an "I" or be changed to an "NG" (no grade). However, changing an "I" to an "F" would imply the student did complete the course work but failed to understand the subject matter. An "I" or "NG," on the other hand, would not misinform the person interpreting the transcript and simply means the student did not complete the course. A course needed for graduation credit or as a prerequisite could be retaken or, if in the professional judgment of the teacher there is enough evidence to determine the student's mastery of a subject, an achievement grade could be compiled from the information available at the time the grade was needed. When and whether the student receives a grade and credit should remain the professional judgment of the teacher, based upon reasonable course expectations. The "NG" grade could have a beneficial effect on "at risk" students. The difference between telling students that they didn't finish the course, or that they failed, could be the difference between deciding to continue in school or not.

Elementary and middle schools have an excellent opportunity to be flexible and innovative when reporting student behavior and achievement because, unlike high schools, they are not limited to a letter grade system requested by employers and college admission offices. An elementary report card could include a letter grade which approximates students' achievement for comparison purposes; separately there could be a place to list the incomplete or missed assignments, the tests not taken, the number of late arrivals, absences, and other behavioral information. Parents of elementary students are more likely to attend conferences to receive firsthand behavioral information and are usually more responsive to suggested ideas for learning activities at home. Instead of trying to use one letter to tell the whole story, elementary teachers could have an oral and written reporting system which presents a complete and accurate picture of student achievement and development.

Often students caught **cheating** on exams or **plagiarizing** assignments receive an "F" for their wrongdoing, which is averaged with their other grades or used as the final grade in the course. The problem with this practice is that an "F" connotes academic achievement (or lack thereof) and will be interpreted as such by those who read it. For this reason, educators should approach cheating and plagiarism as a behavioral matter. Focus on the problems which lead up to the act itself and separate this from evaluating achievement. For example, a student caught cheating on an exam could be offered a make-up exam, possibly in another format, or a broad essay question which could be graded quickly and be sufficient to evaluate the students' achievement. Plagiarizing would certainly entail completing another paper covering the same subject. In addition to providing for alternative academic requirements, apologizing to classmates, class discussions, conferences with parents or guardians, and/or counseling sessions communicate to the student that the problem is much deeper and more serious than lowering a grade. With imagination and planning, judicious consequences can function as a deterrent as well as help students learn the rewards of doing their own class work. By separating evaluation from judicious consequences aimed at student misbehavior, educators will be holding together the student/educator relationship as well as protecting student liberties in the difficult arena of cheating and plagiarizing.

Attendance, as previously discussed, is often commingled with the academic grade. If students choose not to attend or are ill, offer an alternative means of learning and then grade accordingly. **Class participation** is often used as a criterion for grading, but is typically limited to those whose hands are raised. To avoid being discriminatory, call on each student the same number of times to allow an equal opportunity for participation. If they miss class, they can participate by completing alternative educational assignments. Grading on effort is appropriate only if there is a place for an effort grade on the report card. Effort denotes a student's behavior, and when combined with achievement would misrepresent the final grade. **Improvement** should not be averaged into a final grade. Improvement implies a change, but it does not provide baseline data or explain to what extent the student improved. **Extra-credit** class work is acceptable if it is relevant and related to the achievement reflected in the meaning of the grade. Grades in **advanced** or **college preparatory** courses should be modified to reflect the overall achievement of the advanced student, or schools will run the risk of advanced students choosing lower level courses to assure themselves of high grades required for college entrance and scholarships. Grade modification may also be necessary for some **handicapped students** mainstreamed into regular classes as well as classes offered specifically for them. Grading down for **misspelling** or **poor grammar** in non-language classes raises the question of educational responsibility for teaching communication skills. Writing ability is important to the student's education and should be monitored by all teaching staff, but not necessarily averaged into the final grade in a science or history class. Poorly written papers, for example, could be returned or not accepted until writing standards are acceptable. The final grade should reflect the **final measure of achievement**. Unsatisfactory course work at the beginning of class averaged with demonstrated ability at the end could misrepresent the student's final mastery of the material or skill level achieved.   And finally, **grading homework** begs the question of equal educational opportunity, as well as whose work is being graded. Comparing a student whose home is conducive to study and replete with educational resources with a student whose home life is hostile to learning and devoid of source material is inherently unfair. To alleviate this unfairness, educators could do such things as allow students to get started on their homework before the end of class, to ensure understanding of the assignment as well as providing time to make sure all students feels confident about their ability to do the work. Designate some hours available for individual help before and after school and on the weekends if Saturday school is offered. Encourage cooperation with other students or go so far as forming a homework club. Use homework more to diagnose problems and for practice necessary for mastery than trying to place too much emphasis on averaging it into the final grade. Although time devoted to schoolwork outside class hours leads to a better understanding of the subject being taught as well as to the development of good study habits, it does not necessarily represent valid evidence of individual student achievement.

Every effort should be made to keep grades as an accurate reflection of students' academic achievements for the clarification of those who will ultimately use the G.P.A. The balance between the need for educators to use an achievement grade to control behavior, and students' need for accurate assessment of course work, must tip in favor of students' liberty interests. Consider one exaggeration to make a point. Is it true that all pre-operative patients hope their surgeons' successful completion of medical school was not due to grades inflated by effort and improvement? Again, the issue is not what the educator thinks the grade should mean, **but what those people interpreting the grade believe it to mean.**

Daniel Blaufus, a teacher at Kraxberger Middle School in Gladstone, Oregon, experienced a dramatic change in his classroom as he moved to a more judicious approach to management and grading. The following are his words:

"The most immediate effect of my reading of *Judicious Discipline* is in my classroom management. The entire atmosphere of my class and the relationship I have with my students has been radically changed. My old emphasis of discipline and deadlines has been replaced with compassion, understanding and the best interest of the individual. It's remarkable to me how much I am suddenly enjoying teaching and how much my students are finding me to be an adult to whom they can turn for understanding. There have been times in my years of teaching when individuals have known that I genuinely care about them as individuals, but with a few alterations in approach, I have 125 kids who feel I am really working for them.

"These changes have come about through implementing many of the strategies outlined in *Judicious Discipline*. It has felt so right to tell parents and students that I believe it is important that the course work is completed. When parents come in for explanations of their child's incomplete, my remarks make sense and show profound respect for the student and the subject matter. Every encounter I have had with parents and students has been very positive because the choice is left with them. Not all of them have made up the incompletes, and when the counseling department comes to me to find out what grade the child earned, I give them my best professional assessment of the student's knowledge. I finally feel like a professional educator and not a youth group leader trying to instill all sorts of values and behaviors before I can give a grade."

⚖️

Punishment

Legal Implications

Those who choose to punish students should be knowledgeable about the legal issues related to their decision. For example, punishment must begin with a clear perspective of the **gravity of the offense**. Well-chosen disciplinary measures should be in proportion to the offense and reasonably defensible for the purpose used; i.e., to deter improper conduct, punish, or rehabilitate the student. Age, as well as the mental, emotional, or physical condition of the students, are factors which must be considered when determining reasonable punishments. Punishment must never be used in a way that can be construed as malicious, cruel, or excessive. Student handbooks and teachers must provide **adequate notice** to students, outlining the possible punishment for violations of specific school and classroom rules.

Students have a valid argument when they admit they knew it was against the rules for them to copy another's answers on a test, but were not aware that cheating could result in punishment as severe as expulsion. Punishment as a deterrent or a legal consequence is only as effective as the sufficiency of notice.

Withholding privileges, as opposed to rights, is judicially considered an acceptable punishment. Legally, students have a right to participate in basic curriculum activities as opposed to those considered "extracurricular." For example, a senior who seriously disrupted the school environment on the eve of graduation has the right to graduate on the basis of having met the requirements, but the privilege to participate in the graduation ceremony may be denied as a reasonable disciplinary measure. However, denial of an extracurricular activity may not be arbitrary; it must be reasonably related to student behavior. Because there is a fine line between the two types of school activities, exclusion of a student should not occur without careful consideration and sufficient evidence.

Corporal punishment has long been used to punish students for unacceptable behavior and is still a legal option for administrators who choose to adopt it as school policy. If permitted by state law and authorized by a school district, the administrative procedure should include the following:

1. Parental approval;

2. A due process procedure which includes charges, evidence, and the student's right to be heard;

3. Reasonable administration with moderation, prudence, and consideration of the gravity of the offense, and physical condition and size of the student;

4. Be privately administered apart from the presence or hearing of other students;

5. Be witnessed by a certificated staff member;

6. Be properly recorded and placed on file as a matter of record;

7. Notification to parents or legal guardian.
Parents or guardians who choose not to allow their children to be administered corporal punishment should be offered an alternative form of discipline.

Most state laws allow educators to use **reasonable physical force** upon a student when and to the extent an educator reasonably believes it is necessary to maintain order in the school or classroom. The situation occasionally occurs when attempting to remove a disruptive student from a class or defending against an attacking student. Whether reasonable physical force was used is always a question for the jury and will turn upon whether the force employed was necessary and proportionate to the risks presented in each case. Punishing students at school for participating in **activities occurring off-campus** must be reasonably related to the efficient and well-ordered operation of the school. For example, a student who lets air out of a teacher's car tire at a shopping mall on the weekend could be answerable to school officials on Monday morning.

Educational Problems

Punishing the group for the acts of one student is seldom successful and often results in both student and teacher frustration, as well as nudging the periphery of innocent students' liberty interests. If the culprit cannot be identified with reasonable inquiry, it is better to desist and take appropriate action to prevent the incident from recurring. To **reprimand** and **demean** students in the presence of their classmates not only has a detrimental effect on their self concept, but often intensifies into a spectacle of human emotions and verbal exchanges. Confidentiality and liberty are negated by the public release of professional information and personal feelings. Punishing students for the **actions of their parents** or others over which students have no control, leads to a feeling of injustice and hopelessness that comes from being caught in the middle. For example, students reprimanded for tardiness due to the negligence of parents to wake them creates confusion and a "What's the use of trying?" attitude. Before **keeping students after school,** consider the foreseeable problems related to their returning home safely. The embarrassed faces on fidgeting students sitting **outside classroom doors,** sheepishly eyeing those passing by, is a constant reminder of the effect public banishment has on students' self-concept: a critical determiner of future successes and liberty interests. Whenever possible, speak with students privately and avoid the public exercise of authority or exaggerating the students' misdeeds and mistakes by constantly bringing them up again and again. Writing students' **names on a blackboard** can be equally detrimental and have the same psychological effect as spanking students in front of the class or placing them in the hall. In most cases the student has been tried and convicted by the teacher without their due process rights of notice of the rule they violated, evidence against them, and opportunity to explain themselves. Not allowing students to participate in class because they **do not have a pencil or school supplies** is not consistent with their right to an equal educational opportunity. Allow students to "borrow" school supplies for the class period as a way of modeling the importance of being prepared while still permitting the student the benefit of classroom activities. Punishing students by **requiring more academic work** discredits the intrinsic value of learning as well as the subject matter involved. Avoid using subject matter and learning activities as a form of punishment. It is ironic that the same rooms used to stimulate and encourage learning are assigned as **detention** rooms to punish misbehaving students. A student doing detention is the same as a prisoner in jail. Even our nation's penal institutions have changed their name and thinking by referring to themselves as corrections facilities. Renaming detention rooms to correction room or problem solving room, as some schools have done, would be a first step in bringing about an educational approach to resolving behavioral problems.

I do not recommend punishment. The repercussions are simply antithetical to the goals of professional educators. I recommend judicious consequences that begin with education and encouragement, proceed through counseling and conferences, and eventually move as a last resort to reassignment of the student to a more appropriate educational environment. The students' responses to each approach will help educators understand student goals and motives as well as providing feedback needed to indicate success or an appropriate next step that must be taken. I find, however, that many educators feel the need of a professional response through punishment for some infractions. It is for those teachers and administrators I have provided the information and issues contained in this section.

⚖️

Property Loss and Damage

Reasonable rules protecting public school property seem to be well accepted by students. If a problem occurs, it is usually because of a lack of communication resulting from whether or not students have received **adequate notice** that their actions were damaging to school property. For example, students who are allowed to put their feet on chair seats at home may find nothing wrong with doing it at school, or wood shop students who have not been instructed otherwise might use chisels as screwdrivers because they have seen this done by one of their parents. Identifying and discussing foreseeable problem areas at the beginning of class will undoubtedly lessen the likelihood of student misunderstanding and embarrassment resulting from lack of information. Adequate notice and proper instruction are essential to a fair and reasonable school policy designed to protect property from loss and damage.

Judicious consequences for **damage to public property** should be consistent with and proportionate to the severity of the loss incurred and the students' genuine feelings of remorse. **Public service,** for example, has traditionally been accepted by judges as an appropriate lesson for public offenders. Options educators might employ to help students learn respect for the property of others could be: making "Keep the School Clean" signs for display around school; picking up litter around the school; helping with a community cleanup project; or teaching younger children the value of protecting school and personal property. Equipment or books not returned could result in loss of privileges associated with the class or activity. For example, a football jersey not returned at the end of the season would bar the offending student from participation in other extra curricular activities until returned or paid for. Property taken from **other students** could be followed with its return or reimbursement as well as an apology for the indiscretion. In most states parents can be held accountable by law for the intentional acts of their children and required to reimburse the school, up to a specified limit, for the damage caused; i.e., vandalism, stolen property, etc. Students who have accumulated **large debts** and refuse to pay could face appearances in small claims court, if the school chooses to pursue the matter.

The loss or damage of any **student's personal property** is always a matter of concern for public school officials. Students and parents should be informed that bringing personal items to school could result in their loss or damage, possibly due to the behavior of others. Both parent and student should know every effort will be made to help students care for their belongings, but that schools do not have adequate supervisory staff to insure the safety of students' personal effects. A solution for students might be depositories designated in the office or each classroom for those who choose to bring personal items to school for class projects, show and tell, for personal expression, or enjoyment during free time. By cautioning students and parents about the problems of protecting their personal effects and providing safe places for their personal property, school authorities are balancing students' individual interests with a workable administrative practice.

Rules relating to school and personal property should be

perceived by students as guidelines for responsible behavior; with educational consequences designed for the purpose of changing attitudes and goals. This requires educational leaders teaching and promoting an attitude of pride in the facilities and respect for the property of others. Class discussions, posters around school, and occasional complimentary and encouraging statements are a few more ways to help students build and maintain good feelings about their school. A positive educational approach designed to create a protective and caring attitude among students for school and personal property will, in the long run, be far more effective than playing out a punishment model.

⚖️

Speech and Expression

To write, interpret, and enforce **dress and appearance** rules is often a frequent source of perplexing and difficult management decisions. Control over student clothing is often attempted with a plethora of rules covering unacceptable appearance including such attire as: short skirts, long skirts, shorts, short shorts, hats, coats and jackets in class, knickers suits, jump suits, coveralls, frayed trousers or jeans, shirttails outside pants, tie-dyed clothing, tank tops, bare midriffs, plunging necklines, jewelry, clothing with slogans, pictures, or emblems, and, of course, hair--style, color, and facial. In addition to unacceptable appearance, schools often mandate that students wear such clothing as: socks, shoes, shirts, and bras. The problem with using the "exhaustive list" approach is that rules must constantly be rewritten as fads and styles change. The student, for instance, who is suspended for wearing one white glove in school, *a la* Michael Jackson, might find gloves added to the updated list of disruptive dress.

Schools should have one broadly written rule communicating the importance of dress and appearance appropriate to an educational environment. The message here is one of respect for the students' ability to decide reasonable appearance in a school setting. Students, who school officials believe are going beyond reasonable bounds, should be handled on an individual basis. Although a vague rule on dress and appearance is not adequate notice to suspend, students should not be removed from school for inappropriate dress until all educational, counseling, and conference avenues have been exhausted. If suspension becomes necessary, this educational approach will provide sufficient notice.

While it is true that students have some First Amendment rights of speech and expression in public schools, they do not enjoy those rights in their homes. With this in mind, a good first step in matters of questionable student dress and expression is to contact the home. Inform the student's parent or guardian their child's appearance may be deviating from their family values and encourage them to handle the situation. If the parent or guardian agrees and rectifies the problem, the matter is closed. But if a parent comes to school wearing the same clothing that led to inquiry, back down unless the student's appearance is **pervasively vulgar** or **clearly inappropriate** for the age and maturity of the student body. If student dress and appearance are statements of family values, it only makes sense to work cooperatively and rationally with parents and guardians on issues of acceptable school appearance. **Public displays of affection**, for example, are often difficult to control, but knowledge that the home will become involved in cases of questionable behavior at school may cause students to think twice about the way they reveal their feelings in public.

Occasionally students or teachers feel uncomfortable or complain about the **actions or appearance of another student**. In such cases, help the students realize that an individual's appearance may not only be acceptable at home, but is a self-expression protected by the First Amendment. We all should work to understand these actions from a constitutional perspective and, in turn, learn to appreciate our nation's rich cultural diversity and the individual differences among families in today's society.

Examples of student speech and expression that are protected in the public schools include the right of students not to participate in the *Pledge of Allegiance*. Although students enjoy the right to read about **ideas** contained in school books, they lose this right if the book is judged to be **pervasively vulgar**. Students who bring their **own literature** to school or who **display pictures** and posters in their lockers should be given notice that these materials must meet the test of their family values as well as the school's test of pervasive vulgarity.

When requiring certain dress and appearance, use one of the four compelling state interest arguments as a rationale for the rule. Legitimate educational purpose may be the reason to require specified dress such as **wearing robes** at graduation or musical performances, or white shirts and blouses for team members on game day. Health and safety might be a compelling state interest to require students to **wear shoes** in school or appropriate **protective gear** when participating in certain sports or activities. The mental health of students is the reason used to limit **lewd and indecent** expression on clothing as well as in speech and around the school. **Gang dress and activities** would be an example of expression not allowed because of the potential for a serious disruption.

Insubordination and open defiance of a teacher's authority violates the law in most states, and often results in suspension or expulsion. Although removal from school is legal, the student/educator relationship would encourage a broader interpretation and approach to the problem. Experienced educators have learned not to personalize students' obscene language or insolent attitudes directed at them, but to perceive such behavior as symptoms of other problems. A student, for example, who calls a teacher an "SOB" during class may be reacting to something that happened at home or during the lunch hour with another student. The visceral reaction of an angry finger pointed toward the door and a "You're history!" should be replaced by a more judicious response such as "Do we need to talk about this now or can it wait until class is over?" The teacher would not be backing down or condoning the student's language, but exemplifying a professional demeanor and the empathy needed to help a student who is having a bad day. Removing defiant students from the educational setting takes them away from educators, counselors, and administrators who are in a position to help them learn habits and manners of civility. A physician, for example, continues to seek a cure for truculent patients who refuse to take their medicine and does not consider banishing them from the hospital as a viable alternative to proper treatment. Cooperative efforts with parents, guardians, and other professionals, especially those enjoying good rapport with the student, should be played out before considering reassignment to another educational setting. **Profane language, indecent gestures, and bigoted statements** are problems similar to those mentioned above and could be handled in the same manner.

Educators should encourage independent thinking and a vigorous exchange of students' ideas by providing bulletin board space in prominent places throughout the school for **free speech activities.** Begin with a large one, near the school entrance, as well as one in every classroom. It is important for students to feel they have a public forum to speak out on issues of personal interest and public concern. By providing free speech bulletin boards, school authorities are balancing student rights with the school's need to control the reasonable time, place, and manner of student expression. Designated student bulletin boards would allow school officials to restrict daily announcements and other bulletin boards solely to school sponsored events and activities.

In the words of the *Tinker* decision: "...this sort of hazardous freedom...this kind of openness...that is the basis of our national strength...must be balanced with states' interests in providing an educational environment free from serious disruptions." Teachers and administrators should not act precipitously or without serious deliberation on issues of student speech and expression. Student, parent, guardian, and educator cooperation may be the most judicious course to follow in matters of student expression. Professional educators have a duty to help students learn the responsibility that goes with being themselves, as well as to develop in them the patience and understanding for those who are.

Search and Seizure

Occasionally, teachers and administrators have reason to search students who are suspected of concealing such things as books, school equipment, drugs, or the personal property of another student. In most instances the teacher just wants to recover the property, remove a distracting toy from circulation, or return what was taken to the rightful owner. In the past, some teachers have summarily emptied pockets, opened desks, or cleared out lockers in order to locate missing items. This somewhat heavy-handed approach has now given way to students' rights under the Fourth Amendment, which require teachers and administrators to search for and seize suspected contraband and prohibited items in a fair and reasonable manner.

The **Fourth Amendment** of the United State *Constitution* forbids "unreasonable searches and seizures" by government officials and provides that warrants "describing the place to be searched, and the persons or things to be seized" can be issued only "upon probable cause." This amendment is applicable to school situations when a state or federal criminal prosecution based on evidence obtained from school premises and the involvement of school authorities occurs. An illegal search will likely bring into play the exclusionary rule used by courts to exclude evidence illegally seized. Although some courts have applied this rule to school disciplinary procedures, the trend is away from excluding fruits of an illegal search at expulsion hearings.

This process for reasonable searches has been interpreted for public school educators in the United States Supreme Court case of *New Jersey v. T.L.O.*, 105 S.Ct. 733 (1985). Justice White, writing for the majority opinion, analyzed what is reasonable under the Fourth Amendment in a public school situation and found that such a determination requires balancing "the individual's legitimate expectations of privacy and personal security" against "the government's need for effective methods to deal with the breaches of public order." The majority of the court determined that the warrant requirement was "unsuited to the school environment" and held "that school officials need not obtain a warrant before searching a student who is under their authority." The court further stated that in its place "the legality of a search of a student should depend simply on the **reasonableness**, under all the circumstances of the search." Reasonableness involves a two-fold inquiry: **First**, one must consider whether the action was justified at its inception and, **second**, one must determine whether the search as actually conducted was reasonably related in scope to the circumstances which justified the initial interference. Although the Fourth Amendment states the government must have "probable cause" to search, the standard which is now applicable to public schools is **"reasonable cause"** which requires considerably less evidence. By applying a lower standard for educators, the Supreme Court balanced the rights of students to an unreasonable search with the custodial responsibility school officials have for the supervisory and educational demands of public schools.

In applying these legal standards, the important question facing educators is "...what evidence is relevant and necessary to determine reasonableness?" White's opinion helped answer this question when he stated that, "...such evidence need not conclusively prove the ultimate fact in issue, but only have any tendency to make the existence of any fact that is of consequence to the determination of the action more probable or less probable than it would be without the evidence." To meet the first half of this two-fold inquiry, the teacher must have some evidence or reasonable suspicion that a student is hiding or has possession of something prohibited before initiating a search. For example, to allow an administrator to open all the students' lockers just to "see what might turn up" would, of course, be without reasonable cause at its inception, and thus be in violation. However, several students who reported to an administrator that they saw a school tape recorder in another student's locker would provide at its inception the reasonable suspicion necessary to make a legal search, regardless of whether or not the recorder was found.

The second part of the two-fold inquiry relates to the scope of the search, or "now that I have reasonable suspicion there may be school property concealed in a student's locker, how far can I take a legal search?" If the recorder is not found in the locker, can a search of the student's car in the parking lot, pockets or purse, or a strip search of the student be carried out? **Scope** encompasses the reasonableness of the depth and breadth of the search which must be plausible and logical in accordance with the circumstances presented. It also is a question about the degree of intrusiveness connected with the search. The highest degree would be a strip search--the lowest would be the search of an inanimate object such as a locker. Therefore, when searching a student's person, a higher degree of suspicion and danger are required than that of searching a car or locker. The Supreme Court stated that the search should not be "excessively intrusive in light of the age and sex of the student and the nature of the infraction." Reasonable cause or suspicion both at the inception and during the scope of the search will be weighed carefully when determining the legality of a public school search and seizure.

Random searches of student lockers and desks are legal if a teacher can show a compelling state interest to conduct a blanket search. For example, at the end of each semester many school officials conduct searches to locate lost or misplaced school property as well as clean up such health hazards as spoiled food and spilled drinks. This type of search would clearly fit under the state's interest in maintaining its property. It is very important, however, to advise students there will be periodic searches and notify them in advance when and for what reasons the searches will occur. This open and straight forward approach not only adds to the integrity of good administrative practice in the eyes of the students, but reduces student suspicions that administrators are "sneaking around behind them." Whenever possible, **have students present** when conducting the search. If students are not present, administrators risk possible accusations of taking something else from a locker or desk, or just invading a student's privacy. When students cannot be present, ask another adult to witness the search and record the property seized. Although students may lose some of their rights of privacy, they do not give up their **right to notice.** If something is found to be missing during class, a **random search** of all students before they leave the room could be a constitutional infringement on their rights. However, if there is reasonable suspicion that a specific student was concealing someone else's property, searching that one student would be admissible.

Health and safety are compelling state interests which permit a blanket search of all lockers in the event of a **bomb threat.** If something illegal is found in plain view during an emergency search, it would not be unreasonable for school authorities to seize it. In the case of a clear and present danger, such as a bomb threat, we can all expect to lose our constitutional rights until the danger has subsided. The blanket search ban has also been applied to **extra-curricular activities,** such as searching the luggage of band members before they leave on concert tour. On the other hand, health and safety may be used someday as a compelling state interest to require urinalysis of athletes if they choose to participate in athletics. Athletes high on drugs create a risk not only to themselves, but to all the other participants. Except for emergencies, serious injuries, and periodic searches for school property, random searches of students or their lockers is not advised.

A common practice in education is **taking student property** which is disruptive or not allowed by school rules. Squirt guns, knives, or new "fads" that come along are occasionally taken and held for the student until the end of the school day. Although these items may be properly disallowed, a teacher or administrator who confiscates property and does not return it within a reasonable period of time is similarly blameworthy by committing a "tortious taking of another's chattel." Students' personal property should be returned as soon as possible, with the exception of illegal items and dangerous weapons.

Illegal drugs, firearms, or contraband should be turned over to law enforcement authorities. Ask the law enforcement officer for a receipt listing the items submitted; it could protect you from the embarrassment of accusations that you kept the student's property for yourself. Also consider **giving receipts to students** when you take their property. Providing a student with a receipt has the look of professionalism and the appearance of valuing student's property. A former student of mine, a second grade teacher, reported that until she began giving receipts, she had not realized that by taking toys from students, she was modeling exactly what she was teaching her students not to do: taking things from other people. By issuing receipts, however, she found herself teaching and exemplifying respect for school and personal property. She reported that it had an immediate affect on how students treated each others' belongings as well as their school books and building facilities.

Students who **refuse a reasonable request** to relinquish something they are concealing must be handled with caution. Wrestling students to the floor in order to search pockets or purses may not only result in injury, but be construed later as unreasonable force. Teachers confronted with this situation should not attempt to physically search or seize property, but rely on the assistance of other professionals to conduct the search. In certain cases the search should be handled by law enforcement personnel rather than an educator. As in other confrontations, the best approach to manage uncooperative students might be to bring in their parents or guardian, someone who has the student's confidence. In dangerous situations rely on the expertise of law enforcement personnel.

Although educators are given wider latitude in student searches than are police, it is not a license to search randomly or invade the privacy of students. The *T.L.O.* case has provided very clear guidelines and all the authority necessary to manage successfully a safe and secure educational environment. Teachers and administrators who understand and apply Fourth Amendment concepts judiciously should experience few complaints from students and parents.

⚖️

Press

The First Amendment freedom of the press clause was set forth to prohibit **prior restraint.** Simply stated, our government does not have the legal authority to mandate in advance what anyone may or may not publish. If a person's publication injures another, remedy is a civil action for libel. Publishing material which advocates the violent overthrow of our government or which is obscene may result in a criminal prosecution. Civil and criminal actions both may supervene the publication, and wrongdoing will be decided on the merits of each situation. The freedom of the press question which faces public school officials is whether prior restraint can legally be applied to student publications.

As a general rule, students enjoy only some **substantive due process** rights in the area of school-sponsored student publications, primarily because of their age, impressionability, and the fact they cannot be held legally liable for what they publish. Their substantive rights allow for **some prior restraint,** but it must be reasonably imposed.

The Supreme Court in the *Hazelwood School District v. Kuhlmeier,* 108 S.Ct. 562 (1988) used legitimate educational purpose as a rationale for prior restraint of school-sponsored student publications. The Court declared: "...we hold that educators do not offend the First Amendment by exercising editorial control over the style and content of student speech in school-sponsored expressive activities so long as their actions are reasonably related to legitimate pedagogical concerns." In broad dictum the Court suggested three goals: "that participants learn whatever lessons the activity is designed to teach, that readers and listeners are not exposed to materials that may be inappropriate for their level of maturity, and that the views of the individual speaker are not erroneously attributed to the school." *Hazelwood*, however, does not apply to all student expression that happens to occur on school grounds, only to school-sponsored or curriculum-related publications. It appears that *Tinker's* serious disruption standard will govern "underground" or non-school-sponsored publications.

Although students' substantive due process rights are not co-extensive with those of adults, their **procedural due process rights** are closely guarded by our nation's courts. To restate briefly, the procedural due process rights of students are notice, a fair hearing, and an appeal. Applied to student press matters, **adequate notice** means the material not permitted in student publications must be stated in a manner that is clear, concise, and reasonably understood by the students. **A fair hearing** means that in the event of a disagreement, the students' reasons for publication must be heard and considered before the decision is conclusive. Finally, the student has the **right to appeal** the publication advisor's decision as well as other decisions in the appellate process. Although the law allows reasonable prior restraint, courts show little patience with school authorities who waffle on procedural due process rights in matters of student publications.

Because freedom of the press is such a volatile, and often litigated area of the law, schools should create a **publication advisory board** for the purpose of promulgating guidelines and serving as an appeal body in the event of a student appeal. The membership could include the student editor, the publication's advisor, a student-body representative, a teacher, an administrator, a school board member, and possibly a local newspaper editor. Any appeal to this advisory board or school administrator should be heard without delay, preferably within forty-eight hours to avoid the pretext of administrative delaying tactics. The publication board is only advisory to the building principal's decision, but it offers an informed and politic buffer for many sensitive publication issues which must be decided promptly and fairly each year.

Publication guidelines should include standards of good journalism, emphasizing technical skills in writing and reporting and a statement encouraging students to express their opinions on relevant issues, in addition to a clear and concise list of prohibited subject matter. Publication rules which prohibit obscenity, profanity, libel, ads for any product not permitted minors, political endorsements, demeaning any race, religion, sex, or ethnic group, or material which would cause a substantial disruption of the education process would be specific examples of reasonable prior restraint for student publications. The objective of student publications should be to teach the importance of a strong press in a democratic society and, through example, how an educational administration, faculty, and student body can accept and learn from a free and open exchange of ideas. For example, a student's editorial criticizing the potholes in the parking lot or questioning the quality of the school lunches should be judged on its fairness and accuracy as well as the quality of the author's investigative and reporting techniques. An open and above-board discourse of student reporting and opinion should be encouraged and viewed by the administration as an indicator of a healthy educational environment. If school authorities disagree with the student editor's viewpoint of material presented, the school can easily disassociate itself from the substantive views expressed by inserting a disclaimer in each issue.

Time, place, and manner may be regulated for students who choose to distribute or post **off-campus publications** on school grounds. For example, students who want to distribute flyers stating their opinion on abortion have the right to pass these materials out at school, but not necessarily in a crowded hallway or during classes. Students who object to the ideas being distributed by other students could be encouraged to express their views in a similar manner. Another issue to consider is whether or not students exercise their right to publish and distribute information when they **pass notes** to one another in class. Perhaps by encouraging notes in class teachers might abate some of the disruption now caused by whispering or "under the desk relays," or even improve the concentration of one or two students who feel an urgency to communicate. By discussing the proper time, place, and manner in which to pass notes in class, teachers have an opportunity to turn a negative behavior considered disruptive into a positive writing activity, as well as helping students learn the importance of their responsibility to others. Many teachers who have used this approach have reported that they are also the recipient of notes written in class, often from students who shy away from verbal communication. The *Constitution* and good educational practice both are given real meaning and become true-to-life when something as widespread and enjoyable to students as passing notes is perceived as a matter of civil rights.

There is a delicate balance between responsible student journalism and student's rights to publish their opinions which must be maintained. Unreasonable or heavy-handed censorship of student publications quickly escalates and is often a feature news item in the local press and, on occasion, an administrator's decision to censor can attract national attention. The fourth estate hangs together very well and vigorously guards its freedom from prior restraint and thirsts to champion even the smallest of publication injustices. Administrators must make every effort to avoid confrontations with the press, any press. Make judicious decisions matured by a representative publications committee, assign competent publication advisors, know the law, and learn to appreciate this fundamental right so important to our nation's heritage.

⚖️

Religion

The First Amendment to the *Constitution* provides that, "Congress shall make no law respecting an **establishment** of religion, or prohibiting the **free exercise** thereof." When applied to student rights, this double-edged sword forbids a public school to establish religion, and, at the same time makes every effort to accommodate the free exercise of students' religious practices and beliefs. As simple and manageable as this may appear at first, religion in public schools is one of the most difficult and politically volatile issues facing educators today.

It is important for teachers and administrators to have a clear, workable, and legal perspective on religious discrimination. This begins with an understanding of the application of the tripartite test developed by the Supreme Court over many years and brought together in *Lemon v. Kurtzman*, 403 U.S. 602 (1971). **First,** the statute must have a **secular legislative purpose.** Secular purpose usually translates into legitimate educational purpose when applied to most school issues. **Second,** its principle or primary effect must be one that **neither advances nor inhibits religion.** In other words, school officials must remain neutral and cannot celebrate or advocate a religious point of view, nor can they take a hostile attitude toward religion or impair its worth. **Third,** the statute must not foster an **excessive government entanglement** with religion. There must be a real and ostensible separation between religion and the state. Entanglement matters usually involve control over the use of federal funding and decision-making authority. Rules, decisions, and activities must pass all three tests if they are to meet the constitutional criterion of nondiscriminatory educational practices.

The most effective way to satisfy this tripartite test is to approach religion in public school from an **educational perspective.** Reference or activities related to religion or religious teachings are constitutional if they are intended for a legitimate educational purpose. In 1963, Justice Clark's opinion upheld this concept in *Murray v. Curlett*, 374 U.W. 203 (1963). He stated:

> ...it might well be said that one's education is not complete without a study of comparative religion or the history of religion and its relationship to the advancement of civilization. It certainly may be said that the *Bible* is worthy of study for its literary and historic qualities. Nothing we have said here indicates that such study of the *Bible* or of religion, when presented objectively as part of a secular program of education, may not be effected consistent with the First Amendment.

As professional educators, it is our responsibility to integrate religion's rich and diverse history, traditions, and doctrines into appropriate subject matter areas. As long as school personnel approach religion from an educational perspective, they would be considered responsible educators and their curricula would be perceived as having a secular legislative purpose.

However, if a school activity resembles a **religious celebration,** or if an educator's remarks have the effect of **advocating religion,** then clearly there is religious discrimination and violation of the establishment clause. The line that exists between legitimate educational purpose and religious celebration or advocacy is a fine one, often resting on the educator's intentions and the manner and mode of expression. For example, religious music performed at the "winter concert" may be presented as an entertaining evening of seasonal music representing the educational achievements of students and their ability to perform before an audience. Christmas carols sung could be presented as music Christians sing this time of the year. Whether such a concert comprises a constitutional infringement is usually "in the eye of the beholder" and based largely on where the emphasis is placed: be it staging, programming, styling, or the secular or religious intent of the director.

School prayer, which is common to assemblies and school

activities, has the appearance of advancing religion through
worship and for that reason violates the establishment clause. As
alternatives to opening invocations, many administrators have
substituted meaningful prose or poetry. Although prayer in
schools is unconstitutional, invocations and benedictions in
Congress or at city council meetings are not. Prayers in the
public sector have been held constitutional only if they are used
for a secular legislative purpose. Ceremony, tradition, and its
"solemnizing" function are the most common reasons cited for
secularizing prayer at public functions as well as "simply a
tolerable acknowledgement of beliefs widely held among the
people of this country." These legal arguments have yet to be
applied to elementary and secondary public schools because of
the age, impressionability, and propensity of students to emulate
their teachers. States, however, differ on the question of prayers
at **high school graduation** and inquiry should be made into local
laws. Although school-sponsored prayer is religious discrimination, **a moment of silence** for a legitimate educational purpose
could be legal. For example, many coaches provide a quiet time
before a game for the team to relax or "psych" themselves into
playing well. By having a secular purpose for silence and con-
templation, coaches or others using this practice are neither
advancing nor inhibiting students' free exercise rights to pray
silently during this time.

  Voluntary student prayer and religious study groups meeting
in the public school have also been held in many states to be
unconstitutional. Courts argue that by providing public facilities
and, in some instances, supervision for religious activities before
and after school hours, schools have the appearance of advancing
religion. However, the Federal Equal Access Act passed in 1984
allows high school students a limited open forum before and
after classes, which could not exclude religious activities. This
Act only applies to school districts who choose to adopt it as
policy. Administrators seeking more information about the law
should contact their school attorney and study carefully the pros
and cons of the law before deciding to adopt an open forum

policy. **Students worshiping alone** fall within the intent of the free exercise clause and may be forbidden from practicing their religious beliefs only if school authorities can demonstrate a compelling state interest.

The free exercise clause of the First Amendment allows students, with parental permission, **not to participate** in classes or activities which are contrary to their religious beliefs. Although they may miss class, assigning other course work or completing missed assignments can be expected and would serve to fulfill the school's legitimate educational purpose. Evolution is an example of a controversial subject, and although some students may choose to be excused from its study, those who remain should understand that evolution is a scientific theory and not necessarily fact. Parent-approved **release time programs** for religious instruction off school property for a reasonable period of time each week have been held as a student's right of religious practice under the free exercise clause. Allowing parochial school students to ride **public school transportation** does not violate the establishment clause because busing students to school does not advance religion, but only benefits the state's interest in the health and safety of children.

Students **wearing religious dress** are within their constitutional rights as they freely exercise their religious beliefs. On the other hand, teachers and administrators wearing religious dress or symbols, or who talk to students about their religion, have the appearance of advancing religious beliefs, thereby violating students' rights under the establishment clause. Students who choose **religious themes** for individual art subjects, wood shop projects, musical solos, composition topics, or term papers are exercising their religious freedoms. **Free time** provided to students during class would permit them to read religious material brought from home. Students who wish to **express their religious beliefs** could use the bulletin board space provided for student expression previously referred to in the section titled, "Speech and Expression." **Class decorations** for religious purposes should not be school-sponsored, but space allocated to student expression could be used by students for freely exercising their religious beliefs.

I am reminded of an anecdote told in my school law class by a Jewish woman whose daughter's fifth grade class voted to make and sell Christmas tree ornaments to defray the costs of their class Christmas party. Not only were many class hours devoted to the project, but the students were told they could sell the ornaments only to family members to prevent soliciting sales from strangers. I still remember how the mother's voice trailed off as she concluded by saying, "There really isn't a very big market in a Jewish family for Christmas tree ornaments."

Part of the pain in all aspects of discrimination is the lonely feeling of being "left out." The difference between participating in another's celebration and in a legitimate educational experience can be very subtle. To the one who feels outside and alone, it can mean the difference between enjoying and benefiting from school activities or being "turned off by the system." Not unlike other discriminatory practices, religion too can be the source of discipline and learning problems if not handled properly.

⚖

Discriminatory Practices

The Fourteenth Amendment, from which all discrimination laws emanate, states in part, "...nor deny to any person within its jurisdiction the **equal protection of the laws**." From this brief clause federal and state law makers have enacted enabling legislation which protects students from discrimination based on race, national origin, religion, sex, age, handicap, and marital status. In addition, federal and state agencies have promulgated numerous administrative rules which govern discriminatory practices. This section is not a review of these many laws, but a brief commentary on how an educator's bias and prejudice affects school discipline. Teachers and administrators unaware and insensitive to ethnic, cultural, and status issues, and who are unappreciative of the unique differences among public school students, are more likely to speak and act in ways which result in unequal treatment of students. Only when educators model and teach the qualities of character which make a diverse nation possible, have they met their professional responsibilities as well as the demands of equity in a culturally diverse society.

Educators who seldom stereotype or label others appear to understand and value the background, culture, and unique differences among students in their classrooms. These educators embody qualities which enable them to:

* Expect the same academic achievement and standards of personal conduct from all students regardless of their ethnic group or cultural tradition.

* Avoid comparing or ranking groups with respect to classroom behavior, attitudes, and accomplishments.

* Avoid the use of descriptive terms, stereotyped phrases, or participation in humor that is derogatory or demeaning to any group of people.

* Promptly admit an error in judgment, sincerely apologize, and be willing to learn new perspectives.

* Integrate classroom displays, assignments, and lectures with various people in different roles.

* Make seat assignments, work assignments, line assignments, or play group assignments without regard to race, sex, age, national origin, handicap, spoken language, marital status, or religion.

* Maintain eye contact, smile, stand near, and enjoy all students.

Teachers and administrators who fully comprehend and

believe in the concepts of liberty and equality are going to encounter fewer disciplinary problems and better class participation. Students who feel accepted and understood by those in authority usually have second thoughts about skipping classes or disrupting the educational environment. Educators spend too much time talking and interacting with their class to think they can deceive their students into thinking they hold attitudes which they do not. Few study teachers and administrators more, or know their biases and weaknesses better, than their students. Students are keenly aware that the words educators use are only symbols representing what they want others to believe. Words that say one thing, while gestures and actions another, are often the antecedents of putting a student "at risk." *Judicious Discipline* requires a genuine commitment and conscientious effort to assure all students an equal opportunity for success.

⚖️

Health and Safety

One of the important functions of government is the protection of its citizens. This duty is even more important when government, through its public school personnel, is entrusted with a custodial responsibility for minors. The significance of the matter occasionally surfaces in a lawsuit against the school district, holding those in authority responsible for their negligent acts. While some students may occasionally complain about wearing safety glasses, not being allowed to run in the hallway, or being required to see the school nurse, most recognize the purpose of these rules and, with appropriate reminders, acquiesce. Health and safety policies which are consistently enforced not only protect the students from injury at school but serve to teach good personal habits and redeeming social qualities. In order to be workable and effective, however, rules governing students' health and safety should be:

1. **Well-planned**--Consider what a reasonably prudent teacher or administrator would have foreseen under the same or similar circumstances, periodically inspect for hidden dangers, develop a plan to prevent those foreseeable problems, and follow through with its implementation.

2. **Highly Visible**--Use posters, warning signs, verbal reminders, adequate supervision, and other similar measures to insure adequate notice and control over anticipated problem areas.

3. **Fully Understood**--Use instructional handouts, verbal explanations, notification to parents, tests, demonstrated student ability, and other communication efforts to teach students the proper health and safety rules and procedures appropriate for the activity.

4. **Consistently Enforced**--Use proper supervision, be consistent, and "don't even let the principal enter the shop area without safety glasses."

As a general rule, there should be a direct relationship between the likelihood of injury and the time and effort devoted to health and safety precautions. For example, a shop teacher who demonstrates and uses power equipment or a coach of a contact sport must set aside considerably more instructional time to safety than a teacher in a regular classroom. In classes and activities where there is a likelihood of injury, the educator should:

1. Provide a handout which details the hazards involved as well as instructions to prevent possible injuries.

2. Discuss, demonstrate, and respond to questions until the written material is understood.

3. Allow students an opportunity to participate

and demonstrate their understanding under proper supervision.

4. Make sure all absent students receive the same information and opportunity to participate.

5. Keep accurate records of those who have achieved understanding.

Field trips create the need for even more instruction and concern for proper supervision. Planning for activities off school grounds should take into account the hazards at the site, risks involved in transporting students, the age and maturity of participating students, as well as students with foreseeable problems. Parental notification is essential, not only for legal reasons, but also to inform parents about the students' whereabouts and the educational purpose of the activity. **Students who drive** their own cars for school purposes or to school activities should be required to follow reasonable safety rules. A valid driver's license, adequate insurance coverage, good driving record, and parental permission are examples of reasonable school requirements for those who choose to drive. Given the nature of **extra-curricular activities**, health and safety is the rationale many coaches and activity advisors use to promulgate and enforce rules on matters of curfews, alcohol, drugs, and other personal behaviors of the participants.

Schools in states which do not allow persons under the age of eighteen to **smoke** or **chew tobacco** must prohibit such activities on school premises. Schools without state regulations may choose to ban smoking based on two compelling state interest arguments: health and safety, and legitimate educational purpose. School officials can show smoking is a proven health hazard and a fire safety problem to the smoker as well as others, and that a legitimate objective for an educational system is to maintain and inculcate habits designed to preserve good health among pupils. High school administrators who choose to allow students to smoke and chew at school argue that students are going to smoke somewhere. They feel it is better to get smoking out of restrooms, hallways, and away from other students by restricting smokers to a location which can be adequately supervised and outside the building, preferably out of view of passersby. Administrators receiving public complaints could require parental or guardian permission for students to use the smoking and chewing area. The central issue with smoking and chewing is not necessarily one of student rights, but a pragmatic question of adequate supervision, workable enforcement, and community attitudes.

Teachers and administrators cannot afford to compromise students' health and safety. Looming in the background is always the threat of a time-consuming and thorny lawsuit as the result of negligent health and safety precautions. Good management practice today would include forming risk-management teams, consulting health officials, staying abreast of pertinent literature in the field, attending professional meetings, and seeking competent legal advice. Anticipate and plan ways to handle foreseeable dangers, carry through with proper supervision and instructions, and be consistent with enforcement. If the rule or decision is well thought out and supported by sound professional advice, hold firm and do not waver in matters pertaining to student health and safety.

⚖️
School Fees

Common practice has been to require that students purchase many of their own school supplies and equipment before being admitted to school each fall. These materials range from crayons and specified organizational notebooks for elementary students to uniform clothing for secondary physical education classes. However, many of these requirements changed in the late 1970s when state courts nationally began interpreting their state constitutions as providing for a free public education. Many states followed with legislation which set out what could and could not be charged to students' families. There has been no consistency among these state laws. Some states distinguished between fees for required and elective courses, and others used curricular or extra-curricular classes or activities as a criterion for exceptions. Because of this wide diversity, individual state laws now control and dictate the rules each school must follow.

Nonetheless, a common thread of unlawful discriminatory practices against disadvantaged students and their families weaves its way through all these state laws. Reasonable rules and decisions sensitive to this issue would be in keeping with the spirit of the applicable state laws. Some suggested guidelines are as follows:

> * Avoid rules which require students or their parents to provide any money, materials, or equipment necessary to meet the basic needs of any required class or activity. This would not necessarily rule out discreetly allowing parents an opportunity to provide recommended school supplies and materials if they choose. The difference may be that of some elementary students coloring with their own paper-encased crayons while others are using those paperless, speckled ones procured from a box of in-school supplies. The effect, however, is that all have crayons and are learning to color.
>
> * Health and safety, as opposed to uniformity, should be the required standard for clothing and towels brought from home for use in physical education. For example, cut-offs are all right but belt loops are a safety problem and will have to go.
>
> * School property which becomes the personal property of the student would require reasonable reimbursement to the school for materials and supplies used in the product. A bird feeder made in wood shop, a garment made in home

economics, class rings, annuals, and graduation announcements are common examples of publicly-financed materials which often become student property.

* A reasonable rental fee is often charged for the use of school-owned equipment as well as refundable security deposits in the case of textbooks and other materials. An exception should be an indigent family identified by participation in the federal school lunch program.

* Many schools charge for student body cards, after-school concerts, plays, field trips, sports, and other activities considered to be optional or outside the district's regular school program. Although this is legal in many states, schools should consider these optional activities educational in nature and make every effort to provide them cost-free to all interested students.

Extra-curricular activities often become the focus of discriminatory practices in many schools. To aspiring cheerleaders or football players, the anticipated expense of shoes alone could be a deterrent if students feel their families cannot afford the investment. In order to offset student concerns, many advisors and coaches organize money-making activities to defray individual student costs and, in some instances, use donations to pay for those who cannot. These efforts, while certainly within the spirit of equal educational opportunity, must be handled with discretion.

A graduate student taking my school law class told of a policy in her middle school that required students pay 50 cents admission for school assemblies presented during the school day. Those students without the money were assigned to four classrooms until the assemblies were over and then returned to classes with the other students. It is not surprising that many of the non-attending students expressed to her feelings of not wanting to come to school on assembly days.

Educators must be cognizant of the letter and spirit of these laws and sensitive to the needs of economically disadvantaged students. Separating students by ability to pay is not only discriminatory, but it can be a breeding ground for learning and behavioral problems. While it is good educational practice to provide an opportunity for students to participate in well-planned learning activities and projects, the school activity should not become an end in itself nor a barrier to an economically-disadvantaged student who cannot afford its price.

⚖️

School Records

There are rules and regulations governing student records which must be recognized and put into effect pursuant to the laws of each state. Although state laws vary widely, the Family Educational Rights and Privacy Act of 1974 provides well-defined guidelines which set forth the rights of students and their parents in determining rules and regulations for educational records. In essence, the Act stipulates four major requirements of educational agencies and institutions:

1. They may not have policies which effectively deny parents or eligible students (18 years or older) an opportunity to review and inspect education records.

2. They may not have policies or practices which would deny parents or eligible students an opportunity to challenge content of education records believed to be inaccurate, misleading, or in violation of the students' rights to privacy.

3. They may not have policies or practices which would permit access to or disclosure of information without consent, unless specifically per-

mitted by the Act.

4. They must notify parents and eligible students of their rights under the Act.

The foreboding shadow of interested parents presents another dimension to the maintenance of school disciplinary records, ofttimes opinion-laden and misleading, that heretofore had been available only to professional educators. Because these records are now open to view by parents, guardians, and students at age 18, it is even more important that documentation is in fact true, accurate, and free from editorial comment.

Avoid the use of labels. Labels often obscure and confuse the intended communication and lead to a misunderstanding which in turn could easily infringe upon student liberties. Replace labels with statements from first-hand experiences which describe, detail, narrate, illustrate, or characterize student attitudes and behaviors. For example, a statement that "Bob has sticky fingers," could have more than one meaning. But statements such as "Bob comes to class with sticky fingers on days the school serves cinnamon rolls for lunch," or "I have caught Bob, on several occasions, stealing personal items from students' desks," are descriptive statements that portray vastly different attitudes and personal behaviors. Although "sticky fingers" is a label commonly applied to both those who steal and those whose fingers are covered with sticky substance, the difference between a thief and a messy eater is considerable.

"Susie is lazy." Does this mean she often sleeps in class, does not hand in work on time, is habitually tardy, daydreams, shows lack of interest, does not assume responsibility, or has a learning disability not yet diagnosed? By describing first-hand experiences and allowing others the opportunity to label, educators will not only provide better and more useful information to those interpreting it, but legally stand on much safer ground. If Susie alleges some day that the "lazy" label was a detriment to her getting a job or college scholarship, teachers and administrators will find it far easier to prove a history of late arrivals than trying to remember and provide enough examples of her behavior to convince parents or a court that she was correctly diagnosed and accurately typed as being "lazy."

Avoid rules which **withhold report cards** from students until a fine is paid, a book found, or a uniform returned. The Privacy Act allows parents access to all records which would include the educational information on report cards. If the parent or guardian has access to a student's record, they are entitled, for a reasonable fee, to a copy of it. Include **progress data only** on report cards going home with students and restrict behavioral and attitudinal information to parent-teacher conferences. How many ways, for example, could a "U" in citizenship be interpreted by parents whose only source of information was their child's account of the particulars? **Personal contact** with parents or guardians allows for germane responses to good faith questions and an opportunity for proper elaboration of facts essential to successful communication between the school and the home. **Behavioral information** should be shared with parents or guardians only in the presence of someone qualified to interpret such behavior. Although it is difficult to contact busy or disinterested parents, every effort should be made to speak directly with those concerned about student behavior.

Student records are statements made by professional educators. Avoid unprofessional language and ambiguous statements of student achievement and behavior. Describe in objective terms student behavior and leave labeling to those reading the record. Hanging in the balance are the liberty interests of the students' future opportunities.

⚖️

Parental and Guardian Rights

The question of who decides children's education is balanced between the parents' and guardians' individual rights to raise their children according to their own way of life and the state's compelling interest in shaping an enlightened society capable of self-sufficiency and good citizenship. As a general rule, parents have a right to decide their children's educational needs from among the subjects offered. When parents reasonably disagree with a school's **curriculum requirements,** local authorities should make every effort to excuse their children from part or all of the course in question unless there is a compelling state interest. The state interest usually cited is legitimate educational purpose. For parents who become disillusioned or at odds with public school rules or curriculum requirements, there is always the option of private schools or home teaching. It is, therefore, prudent administration to consider carefully good faith requests for exceptions to required courses and activities.

Many parents and guardians today are **requesting a review** of school activities and curriculum materials which may conflict with their family values. The activities include areas such as values clarification, evolution, sex and death education, drugs, globalism, psychological attitudinal testing, and subject matter described as "secular humanism." The Hatch Amendment of 1978 is cited as the legal basis for these requests. It allows parents to inspect all instructional materials designed to explore "new and unproven" teaching techniques. The Amendment, however, applies only to programs which are funded through the U.S. Department of Education, and not to programs funded through other federal agencies, or state or local sources. Although this federal law affects only a small part of a school's curriculum, the spirit of openness and reasonable exceptions of this law provides an opportunity for educators to encourage parental participation in the education of their children.

Whether the reason is religious, ethnic, moral, or just plain, "We want our children to learn it our way," appropriate educational and astute political decisions must be carefully weighed. Both old and modern courts recognize limits to the power of parents idiosyncratically to determine what their children will study in school. This is especially true where religious claims are tenuous, secular reasons are weak, or the parents or children pressure others to follow their lead in trying to get excused from course work. Except for these limits, parents enjoy strong and consistent legal support to decide what and how their children learn in public schools today.

By encouraging parents and guardians to take an active role in decisions which impact their family values, the educational and disciplinary problems with students are significantly lessened. School rules and decisions not supported by parents or guardians have little effect on students who feel they have license from home to disrupt in ways which coincide with their family values. Not only are teachers directing time away from academics in favor of the disruptive student, but additional time and effort is spent on unnecessary parent conferences. In the final analysis, the balance between family customs and beliefs, and society's need for an educational climate conducive to learning, demands careful listening, clear and thoughtful responses, and judicious decisions.

⚖️

Confidentiality

If there is a vital organ in the body of our *Constitution*, it is the individual's expectation of privacy from governmental action. There is federal legislation, such as the Family Educational Rights and Privacy Act previously discussed in "School Records," and separate state legislation which often provides specific guidelines concerning the confidentiality of student records and conversations between students and certificated staff. Administrators, counselors, special educators, and teachers employed in fields directly impacted by the rules and regulations governing confidentiality must be knowledgeable of and stay current with the applicable federal and state laws. Where these laws do not apply, the principle of professional ethics should prevail. Although ethics do not represent the letter of the law, this sense of professional responsibility and conscience reflects in essence the spirit of our *Constitution*. The following recommendations have their basis in these fundamental principles:

* Consider all conversations with students, faculty, and parents to be confidential from others except those who have a demonstrated professional need to know, or if the information involves a serious question of health and safety: i.e., suicide, abuse, weapons, etc.

* Take steps to insure that students' academic achievement is not viewed or known by others: i.e., code posted grades, use inside or back pages for grades and comments on papers being returned, refrain from verbal comments when returning students' work in class, request permission to display students' papers or art work, etc.

* Avoid comments and visible reactions relating to student behavior in the presence of others. Whispering or conversing outside the classroom door for corrective as well as complimentary purposes demonstrates a concern for student self-esteem and avoids unforeseen problems related to public disclosures.

* Refrain from comparing students in the presence of others or putting misbehaving students on display outside the classroom door.

* Discourage disclosures by others which contain irrelevant and inappropriate information that include confidential data or the private life of others: i.e., statements made during show and tell, gossip about students with others, etc.

* Before touching a student, give thought to possible ramifications: i.e., reactions of abused children, sexual implications, rights to privacy, tort liability, etc.

Student discipline and academic problems are often directly related to a teacher or administrator **disclosing information** which, in retrospect, should have been communicated privately or not at all. For example, telling a student in front of a choir class "You can't carry a tune in a bucket" is hardly the time, place, or manner to diagnose a singing problem. Because of the context of such a remark, and the recognized authority of a music teacher, many students would be discouraged from ever again singing in public. Often statements take the form of a flippant remark or sarcastic comment uttered spontaneously in an effort to be clever or entertaining. Taunting and teasing from other students stemming from a single wanton statement or gesture can have a lasting and often damaging effect on a student's self-concept as well as the initiative and interest they manifest toward school. A principal recently related to me a problem they had with a fifth grader who was absent every Monday. Through some probing she found that every Monday the teacher handed back students' homework graded over the week-end, beginning with the highest grade and moving through the stack to the lowest grade. The student with the attendance problem was always the last to receive his homework assignment.

Occasionally information disclosed in a confidential relationship gives rise to suspected **child abuse**. Abuse is defined by the laws of each state and generally includes neglect, sexual molestation, physical injury, and, in most states, mental injury or emotional abuse. The law requires school personnel to report any suspected child abuse, despite the fact it was a confidential communication, to a law enforcement agency or the government agency with the legal authority to investigate the matter. An abused child is often the result of irrational behavior within the family unit and caution must be used to insure that the focus of the abuse does not shift to an educator blamed by an abuser as the cause of the investigation. Although the law protects the anonymity of the person reporting, good administrative practice would include developing a building guideline for reporting suspected child abuse and establishing an effective working relationship with the agency responsible for the investigation.

Suicide and other life-threatening disclosures are examples of confidential communications which must be reported to qualified school authorities. Many student problems are simply beyond the expertise of educators who are made privy to critical situations. In these cases one-on-one counseling should be avoided by educators and the problem directed to those professionals whose duty and training enables them to work with the troubled student. Although a student may solicit a promise not to tell, in life and death matters or situations that are dangerous to others, the confidential relationship must be abandoned in favor of a professional team approach.

Teachers and administrators sometimes hear confessions by students of past or present **criminal activity,** such as possessing or selling drugs, assault, stealing, extortion, and other similar illegal acts. In the case of only knowing about alleged criminal activity, the teacher is not legally held to disclose the information voluntarily to law enforcement officials. The educator could be legally implicated as an accessory if they act or participate in some way after knowing about the crime. Depending on state laws, school personnel may have to disclose a confidential statement of criminal activity if subpoenaed to testify.

Advising students about abortion, use of contraceptives, conflicts they have with family values, and other similar lifestyle decisions should be avoided. Helping students clarify values is a sensitive matter in most communities, and precautions must be taken not to become the only professional directly involved. Adverse parent reactions, legal ramifications, and students holding the advice blameworthy are possible negative outcomes of imprudent student advising. Although there is no federal law that prohibits **tape recording of conversations,** many states have enacted legislation that require all parties to consent to the recording.

Students who **demand confidentiality** as a condition for relating a personal problem are asking educators to compromise their own personal and professional values. Although there may appear to be a fine line between the law and comforting a disillusioned student, educators must be able to recognize the difference and stay within the legal and ethical limits set forth. Emotional involvement is sometimes difficult to avoid, but every effort should be made to maintain a professional relationship. Convince yourself that you are not the only one that can solve a student's personal crisis, and solicit the help of the best professionals available. Whenever possible educators should walk troubled students to the counselor's office and introduce them to someone who can be of assistance. The personal problems of students are frequently volatile and fraught with unforeseen repercussions. Under very few circumstances would you want to "go it alone."

Although the confidential relationship between student and educator is not commonly associated with student discipline, unprofessional disclosures often precipitate an attitude of mistrust or resentment. On the other hand, educators who show a respect for students' feelings of self-worth and their right to an expectancy of privacy provide the basis for punishment-free learning activities as well as a model environment for maintaining high student self-esteem. Good classroom discipline begins and flourishes when there is a continuing relationship of openness and trust between students and educators.

⚖
Complaint Procedures

Casting its shadow over every public rule and decision is the Fourteenth Amendment right of substantive and procedural due process. Whether or not these rights are stated or written, they are implicit in every public function. How many handbooks, for example, covering student rights and responsibilities enumerate the students' process for appeal concluding with the United States Supreme Court? Frequently the rationale of the administrator is to accord complaint procedures a low profile in the hope that students will be less likely to complain if they remain uninformed. School officials, however, will realize that to encourage student opinion through an accessible and open forum greatly reduces student and parent feelings of frustration, which are often a cause of learning and discipline problems. For many students and their families, just knowing their opinion will be considered or their grievance heard, gives them a positive feeling about school and assures them that the school has placed a high value on students' rights and interests.

The **complaint procedure** should be specific about who decides what, on what basis it will be determined, and when it will be resolved. For example, if classroom rules and decisions are discussed first with the classroom teacher, and if a satisfactory resolution is not reached, then the appeal process should state the title of the teachers' immediate supervisor and the actionable time frames involved. A similar notice of procedure must be followed through to the local board of education. The school board is the legal entity in every district with final authority for all administrative rules and decisions. If an appeal is denied by the school board, students may appeal to either a federal or state administrative agency or trial court, then to an appellate court, and finally, if the justices decide to hear the case, to the United States Supreme Court.

It is important to remember that the complaint process is a viable one and works best if each step is played out properly and none are bypassed. For example, if a parent complains about a teacher to a member of the school board, the board member should refuse to comment directly on the dissatisfaction and courteously refer the parent to the teacher's principal. Undermining the authority of subordinates can dampen team spirit as well as diminish student respect for the capabilities and authority of educators.

The **decision on an appeal** should be decided within a reasonable time period and communicated directly to the parties involved. If possible, speak personally with the student and parents or guardians. Be open about the decision and responsive to valid questions. A conference is good educational practice and has proven to be an effective way to share opinions on sensitive issues. **Academic and behavioral decisions** which affect student liberties and property interests should be left to the wisdom and discretion of professional educators. Student courts or even students who serve on faculty committees which hear appeals often create more problems than the benefits gained from student opinion. Concern about confidentiality, students judging the private lifestyles of other students and their families, and peer pressure to gossip or be swayed are only a few of the uncertainties involved. Although student input in the formulation of rules is very important and educationally sound, decisions made to interpret rules and behavior require the more seasoned, well-informed approach of professional educators.

A balance must be maintained between the students' rights to adequate notice, a fair hearing, an appeal, and the public's need for an orderly and efficient operation of its public schools. Time used to implement these procedures often distracts from other educational responsibilities, but the rewards gained for teaching and providing for students' due process rights are endless, for the students, their families, and our nation's system of government. It is my sincere hope that *Judicious Discipline* may be the moving force effusive enough to give an impetus to all three.

Part IV

Ethics: Beyond the Balance

Ethical practices manifest the conscience of a profession and constitute the acceptable standards of moral and proper conduct. Often professional ethics are referred to as "beginning where the law stops." For example, there is no law against a teacher asking a student in the presence of classmates, "Why can't you be as good as your sister was in this class?" But the ethics of comparing siblings is considered poor professional practice, often precipitating behavior problems which could affect that student as well as the learning climate of the entire classroom. The community esteem of every profession lies in its ethical practices and conduct and this axiom is no less true for educators who are responsible for student learning and discipline.

⚖️

The Student/Educator Relationship

The ethics of classroom discipline are shaped by the educators' perception of their role in the student/educator relationship. If teachers and administrators believe appropriate social interaction and discipline can be learned in the school environment and that it is their mission to put into practice methods and strategies to help students learn and develop attitudes of responsibility, then their professional ethics will reflect a **student-centered** approach. Conversely, **teacher-centered** educators who view classroom discipline as a necessary accommodation for their teaching effectiveness would define ethics in disciplinary matters as student behavior which allows them their right to teach. Or, stated another way, teacher-centered educators may feel their role is not to "babysit" an assigned study hall but to teach their subject matter, while student-centered educators view any student contact as an opportunity to play a part in the growth and development of young people.

An educator's right to teach should be incidental to a student's right to learn. The **right to teach** may be defined as having met state certification requirements--just as an **opportunity to teach** would imply having a teaching position. But a certified and employed teacher has the **responsibility to provide an equal educational opportunity** for all students to succeed regardless of attitudes, abilities, and backgrounds. On the other hand, educators do have rights, but only those which flow from the employee/employer relationship, not from the student/ educator relationship. Public education does not have the right to decide who will be educated anymore than the medical profession decides who will be treated or the legal community determines who will be afforded legal council. **Students have the right** to a public education and teachers and administrators have an ethical, educational, and legal **responsibility** to help all students learn and cooperate in an educational environment.

There must be a style and technique developed to communicate the drama of educational responsibility: an ability to transcend the daily hustle and bustle of interactions between students and educators. This professional level of communication begins by getting the **Self** out of the way. How does one rise above self-interests--through enlightenment and through effort. Enlightenment connotes valuing students' personality and academic development over an educator's personal needs and desires--thereby creating a style whereby egos are mitigated for the purpose of helping every student succeed. Equally important to enlightenment is acquiring the fundamentals of good educational practice as well as the necessary knowledge in fields of study. Enlightenment alone, however, is not enough. Professional style requires a growing period and the seasoning that comes only from practice, practice, practice. Through enlightenment and effort educators learn to lose themselves in the student/educator relationship. Gradually mechanics are mastered, technique is transcended and education becomes a natural creativity. By minimizing self-consciousness, educators experience a feeling of being on top of students' problems and in control of selfish motives. If every thought and move plays off the importance of developing and maintaining the student/educator relationship, the question asked again and again becomes; **how would an educator act upon this matter?** When style and technique are sound, then a level of professional competence and responsibility is attained. Educators begin to sense this level of professional style when it becomes natural to respond to a recalcitrant student by saying, "No matter what you call me or how you act, I am still going to be your educator and do everything I can to help you succeed in school." In the end, a **Professional Self** emerges which becomes the sustaining force behind educational strategies and leadership characteristics needed to successfully resolve learning and disciplinary problems.

⚖️

Positive Ethical Practices

An educator who interacts positively with students and uses a "positive role model" approach is more likely to be effective in maintaining discipline than a teacher who operates from a defensive position. To acquire and maintain a positive approach to discipline is not always easy and often takes years of teaching experience to achieve fully. To state it metaphorically, "Having your cake and eating it too requires the ingredients of law, education, and ethics, mixed and stirred judiciously with firsthand experience and baked at a public school setting until it rises to the occasion."

Whether conscious or subconscious, every professional educator believes in some basic fundamental principles that guide them in their daily activities. From books and articles we have read, classes and workshops we have attended, and the day-by-day interaction with students, parents, and the school community, a professional morality has been shaped in each of us as to how we want to approach our educational responsibilities. I suggest we think and talk to others more about our ethics as a way to constantly remind ourselves of the things we should "always" be doing as educators.

Although I have alluded to ethics many times throughout the preceding pages, I would like to offer the following as ethical principles I have found helpful for me in providing a focus for my energies and priorities in matters relating to the education of my students:

1. **Model responsible professional behavior.** Establishing and maintaining a professional image is important to every profession. Appropriate dress and appearance, good organization, knowledge of subject, preparation for class, beginning class on time, and following through on promises made are only a few examples of model congruence. On the other hand, avoid drinking coffee in class while not allowing students food or drink,

or lecturing from a messy desk about the importance of being neat. Hypocrisy and unbefitting behavior combine to undermine professional integrity and have a negative effect on the efficacy of the student/ educator relationship.

2. **Manifest appropriate personal behavior.** Educators must avoid expressing inappropriate personal opinions and information about their private lives to students and others within the context of the school environment. For example, whether or not a teacher has ever experimented with drugs or how they feel about controversial social issues should be kept as personal matters. Educators serve as role models and risk loss of respect, added discipline problems, and in some cases their jobs as the result of disclosing inappropriate information that unduly influences the impressionable minds of their students. Educators should take the initiative and choose to speak with students about hobbies, activities, and interests which show a personal side and avoid value laden and controversial subjects.

3. **Develop judicious rules and consequences which accept students as citizens.** Management by whim and caprice can lead to embarrassment, alienation, and discipline problems. Educators who seek to understand individual differences among students and thoughtfully balance these differences with the rights of the majority will enjoy a positive relationship with students and their families. As a school counselor I would often use analogies to help troubled parents cope with the adolescent behavior of their children. One such analogy was to suggest to parents they begin treating their teenager as they would a guest in their home. For example, when a guest inadvertently spills food on the floor, help is usually offered and an apology is quickly accepted. Their children, on the other hand, are usually scolded and forced to clean the mess by themselves. What is not understood by many parents is the fact that anger, followed by a lecture and demeaning remarks, is not teaching their children prudent table manners, but how to treat children who make mistakes. The same is equally true for educators. A judicious approach would treat nonconforming students as citizen-guests. Courtesy, dignity, and

respect are all-important to disciplinary style, which is, in many cases, more important than substantive matters.

4. Encourage and model an eagerness for learning and teaching. Just "going through the motions" is usually reflected in student achievement and behavior. Enthusiastic educators fired up about the joys of learning and their subjects are infectious, often making the difference to a student who decides not to drop out, or providing the inspiration to someone planning a career previously thought to be out of reach. Educators who are growing in their subject matter, developing new teaching or administrative strategies, active in professional organizations, and modeling the benefits of life-long learning will continue to experience the rewards of education. These teachers never burn out; their flame just becomes brighter.

5. Focus efforts on motivation, encouragement, and building student self-esteem. Fortunate is the student of an educator who has mastered the art of motivation and encouragement and applies these talents first before moving on to less positive, perhaps ego shattering, methods of discipline. Encouragement is effort that enhances one's feeling of self-worth: effort through words and acts perceived by students as making them feel better about themselves. The ability to encourage and motivate are fundamental tools of good educational practice and the cornerstone of the student/educator relationship.

6. Accept and appreciate the reality that students behave in a manner they believe is in their best interests. For better or worse, students are the best they can be at the time of their behavior. Educators must accept that behavior as honest and sincere before changes in student behavior will occur. For example, telling a student, "I can't help you if you're not going to try," is similar to a lawyer refusing to defend a criminal who refuses to cooperate. Students must be valued at all times as people education serves, regardless of their attitudes, behaviors, or the severity of their problems. An educator who "keeps the faith" in each student's ability to succeed provides that ray of hope vital to every students' feeling they can succeed.

7. **Enjoy teaching and administration and be proud you have chosen education as a profession.** Perceive educational and behavioral problems as challenges you have prepared yourself to meet. Have confidence your skills and abilities will make a difference in the attitude and effort of any student who passes through your doorway. You must know in your heart you are a better educator than students who believe themselves to be learning or behavior problems.

⚖️
Disciplinary Practices to Avoid

As countless educational and disciplinary problems arise each day, it is often difficult to think of a workable approach or keep from losing our tempers as we feel pushed to the wall. I have learned over the years there is not necessarily a "right" approach to every problem. Each situation requires that we come at it from many sides and examine numerous alternatives before making the best decision or taking the most appropriate action. What has proven helpful for me during this process of determining the best approach is to keep in mind the educational practices that are **never** successful. I hesitate to think how many times one unthinking remark or icy stare unraveled months of positive interaction and reinforcement. By the expression on the student's face, I knew I should not have done or said what I did, and I would vow never to do it again. I eventually discovered that by remembering and avoiding these unsuccessful approaches, I not only kept intact my student/educator relationship, but had the time and freedom to be spontaneous and creative in my search for strategies and ideas which eventually proved successful.

With this introduction, I respectfully submit my list of "nevers," and recommend other educators consider starting their own lists to keep with the lists of things we should "always" be doing. As with most of life's lessons we learn well, I still wear the scars as a reminder that I learned most of these the hard way. For this reason, I would like to dedicate the following "nevers" to all my students, past and present, and thank them sincerely for teaching me how an educator should behave.

1. **Never demean a student or class**, especially in the presence of others. It will always diminish students self-esteem. Sarcasm meant to be clever, or a degrading statement flaunting power or intellect, always hurts students and often is the beginning of an adversarial relationship. Most of us learned to accept being put-down from well-meaning parents, as a way of teaching responsibility and "just keeping the kids in line." I found in demeaning students that not only did I damage both professional and personal relationships, but, no matter how often or hard I tried, I could never fully regain the student's or classes' confidence and respect.

2. **Never send students out of your classroom**; accompany them to the hallway in order to learn more about the problem. I always viewed the problem differently after hearing the student's side of the story, which made my next decision a better one than if we had not discussed it. The message you send to the class is a professional one of concern and willingness to work with individual problems, rather than to summarily send them on to someone else.

3. **Never compare students**, especially siblings. I did not do this more than once, and will never forget the way the student looked at me just before turning his eyes away. Students want to be judged on their own merits and not be thrust by their teachers or administrators into the shadows of others.

4. **Never demand respect**; give it to your students. I discovered by giving it away it was returned to me many times over. Respect, not unlike love, implies the feeling of another which cannot be taken or demanded and is only accorded to another.

5. **Never be dishonest with students**. If I said I would do something, I made every effort to do it. If not, I found an apology was greatly appreciated. A teacher who is open and

authentic earns the trust and respect essential to the student/educator relationship.

6. **Never accuse students of not trying** or ask students to try harder; always help them try again or suggest another way. I found accusatory and judgmental statements diminished relationships and had the opposite effect of making the students not want to try at all. Students want learning situations with encouraging positive approaches, not negative experiences which alienate and discourage. Accept the students' efforts as genuine while communicating a message of faith in the students' abilities to learn. This may appear to be a subtle difference, but the students' reaction will be one of renewed effort and interest.

7. **Never get into a power struggle.** Sometimes power struggles are difficult to avoid, but with common sense and patience I became quite good at sidestepping them. If you sense a power play is developing with students, begin to taking your sail out of their wind and anchor yourself with a long tether. These are no-win situations, and should be handled privately at a later time, through individual discussions and mutual agreements. Students rarely defy educators who they feel are on their side and a friend of theirs in the educational process.

8. **Never flaunt the fact you are the teacher and they are the students.** I would do this during my first year as a teacher whenever I felt insecure. I soon realized this decision was made when I was hired and that I did not have to brandish it about at the first sign of conflict. Students usually know when they have messed up and do not need an educator preaching about it. They need a teacher and a friend who will help them recover. I discovered that if students feel you are sincerely making every effort to help them learn, they will try very hard to help you succeed as a teacher.

9. **Never become defensive or lose control of your feelings.** Do not let your pride get out of hand and diminish your personal and professional qualities. Remarks made during the height of emotional anxiety usually cause frustration and embarrassment for the student and regret for the teacher's part. Take a deep

breath, be silent for a moment, and calmly think through a solution that is devoid of emotional overtones. I found that if I were wrong, acknowledged my error, and apologized sincerely, I was considered an upfront teacher with human frailties and suffered very little loss of personal or professional respectability.

10. **Never use fear and intimidation to control students.** I would fall back on this approach when I ran out of workable ideas or felt pressured by the situation. I finally recognized that fear and intimidation appeared to work in the short run, but its long range effects were unpredictable and often gave rise to other problems. Bitter feelings and sullen attitudes would develop and students became very inventive in the circuitous ways they tried to get back at me for hurting them. I learned to back off until I could think of a positive approach to the problem.

11. **Never punish the group** for the misbehavior of one of its members. I learned that more often than not the culprit enjoyed the group punishment and the innocent students blamed me for punishing them. Retreat as gracefully as you can if you find yourself in this box, and find another way to handle the situation next time.

12. **Never act too quickly** with a disciplinary matter. When I would "shoot from the hip" I invariably said and did things I later regretted. I found that by coming around the problem and avoiding the direct-hit approach, errors could be easily corrected and the possibility of both of us saving face was frequently the factor that turned the corner. Unless you have had good results in the past, or you are certain that what you are doing is going to work, patience and time can be a great ally.

13. **Never say "this is easy."** I discovered these three little words intended to motivate and encourage became a monkey on the backs of students who felt insecure about their abilities, as well as those who felt secure, but needed feedback that what they were doing was something more than "easy." As I learned more about the insecurities associated with students' learning problems and personality development, I soon developed other approaches trying to understand the task more from a student's viewpoint

than my own. This approach was perceived by students as my being interested in **their** feelings of success and had an immediate effect of bolstering their confidence. We must appreciate the fact that all students do not share our interest and ability in school or in our subject matter areas.

14. **Never say "you will thank me someday"** as a rationale for something that is perceived by students as not to make sense or have any immediate purpose. I learned that attempting to justify what I was doing by lecturing about future benefits had little effect on motivating and encouraging students. If learning and good behavior had meaning here and now, I did not have to use threats of future difficulties. Make class inviting to all students with interesting and challenging teaching styles designed to meet everyone's learning and personality needs. Educators should want to be "thanked" after each day of class as well as "someday" in their future.

15. **Never think being consistent means treating all students alike.** I was always told that one of the characteristics of a good teacher is being consistent. It took a few years and numerous bad decisions before I stumbled upon what consistency means to good educators. Consistency in education, I have concluded, is being able to identify individual differences among students day after day and provide the professional specialization and skills needed to help all students achieve success. Students realize they have different needs and goals and regard highly the teacher who understands that the same method of teaching and discipline should not be applied to every student. Take the time required to know your students and learn to appreciate and judiciously manage their individual differences.

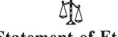

Statement of Ethics

Draft your own statement to post in your classroom or office, outlining the ethical basis which supports your style of management and teaching. Post it beside your classroom and building rules. Not only will students and parents have notice of your rules, but they will also know something about your disciplinary philosophy style. Allow room for additions which you may include throughout the school year. This open-ended document illustrates the fact that experience is a good teacher and communicates to others you are open and responsive to learning new approaches. Spend class time discussing your professional ethics and philosophy of discipline. Allow students an opportunity to react and express their opinions. In addition to setting the tone for your disciplinary style, students can learn the ofttimes subtle distinction between law and ethics.

⚖️

Student Ethics

As students learn more about ethics and understand their importance in our society, suggest they compose their own "Ethics of Student Behavior." Help them prepare their list of behavioral goals and principles to guide them in matters of educational and disciplinary actions. Suggest topics such as honesty, promptness, initiative, cooperation, responsibility, concern for others, and ways they can help educators succeed. Other examples would be to discuss how they would treat a student who was being disciplined, how students themselves should accept and learn from judicious consequences, and how to separate their misbehavior from that of being accepted as a person of value. Student opinion and interaction about "principles of style" relating to disciplinary actions could be a profitable learning experience, as well as an acknowledgement of shared responsibility and authority. When the student document is ready, with space for additions, post it next to the rules and your statement of ethics. These official looking pronouncements of law and ethics will act as a reminder to all about their mutual goals and ideals for an exemplary school environment.

Using the same interactive approach she used to develop her rules, the following is the statement of ethics Margie Abbott's fourth graders (previously mentioned in the "First Day of Classes") decided to try to achieve. They posted them near their rules to show how both are interrelated and equally important:

1. We would like to be treated with respect.
2. We would like others to be considerate of our feelings.
3. When papers are displayed, we would like to have all class members' papers displayed, not just a few.
4. We would like to be treated equally, but not the same.
5. We want to be able to trust our teacher to give matching consequences when a rule is broken, and not embarrass us.
6. We would like the people in the class to be responsible for themselves.
7. We would like the people in the class to be considerate of our ideas and opinions.
8. When we disagree with someone, we can be polite and not explode.
9. We want people to help people when they need it, but not give the answers. (No help on tests.)

In summary, the ethics of any profession are at best fragile and difficult to manage when put into practice. Because morality is a matter of character, educators must have a general concern for ethical behavior to begin with. As the doors to classrooms close behind teachers beginning their classes, who is to know if responsible professional ethics will be used to guide all educators' actions and decisions? For ethics to be viable, there must be a continuing, on-going moral and ethical inquiry. When educators wear well the mantle of the profession, their biases and personalities take a secondary status to the problems and people they serve. To our students we appear larger than life and, therefore, must personify a model of professional demeanor. It is imperative that we develop and keep alive the student/ educator relationship. If a student has little or no family influence, by default the educational system becomes that influential family. In its final analysis, a teacher's classroom is the student's world.

Bibliography, Resources and References

Legal

I have focused primarily on the synthesis of school law, proven educational practice, and ethics, and have made a conscious effort to minimize legal language and references. This book is not intended as a legal resource, but rather as a guide to judicious rules and decisions based on legal precedent. Teachers and administrators seeking a legal opinion should always consult the attorney that will be representing them if litigation from that opinion should occur.

To teachers seeking more legal information and materials for classroom use, I recommend sending for the West Publishing Company's catalog for law-related textbooks. They publish an

excellent series designed for classroom use from grades two
through twelve:

West Publishing Company
Attn: Law-Related Education
58 W. Kellogg Blvd
P.O. Box 64779
St. Paul, MN 55164

Because laws can change quickly and dramatically, it is
essential for administrators and teachers to keep themselves
current. I recommend the National Organization on Legal
Problems of Education as a resource. Its monthly publication
summarizes recent court cases and makes available well-written
articles, books, and collections of legal issues in education. This
is an indispensable reference for every school administrator and
should be accessible to interested classroom teachers. Membership is about $75.00 a year:

NOLPE
3601 Southwest 29th Suite 223
Topeka, Kansas 66614
913-273-3550

Several other books on the subject I have found informative
are as follows:

Editors of *Deskbook Encyclopedia of American School Law*.Infor-
    mation Research Systems, P.O. Box 409, Rosemount, Minn.
    55068 (published yearly).
Kern, Alexander and M. David Alexander. *The Law of Schools,
    Students and Teachers in a Nutshell*. West Publishing Co.,
    1984.
Kirp, D. L. and D. N. Jensen. *School Days, Rule Days*. Falmer
    Press, 1986.
Yudof, M. G., D. L. Kirp, T. V. Geel, and B. Levin. *Educational*

Policy and the Law, Second Edition. McCutchan Publishing Co., 1982.

⚖

Educational

There are many books and classroom management models available to educators which do not punish students, but take a positive approach to changing goals and attitudes. I recommend the following resources as references, methods, and strategies which fit well within the framework of *Judicious Discipline*:

Briggs, Dorothy C. *Your Child's Self-Esteem*. Doubleday, 1970.

Combs, Arthur. *A Personal Approach to Teaching: Beliefs That Make a Difference*. Allyn and Bacon, 1982.

Combs, Arthur. *Helping Relationships*, 3rd Ed. Allyn and Bacon, 1985.

Craig, Eleanor. *P.S. You're Not Listening*. NAL, 1973.

Dewey, John. *Democracy and Education*. Free Press, 1966.

Dreikurs, Rudolf. *Psychology in the Classroom*. Harper and Row, 1968.

Dreikurs, Rudolf. *Discipline Without Tears*. Dutton, 1974.

Dreikurs, Rudolf. *Maintaining Sanity in the Classroom*, 2nd Ed. Harper and Row, 1982.

Faber, Adele and Elaine Mazlish. *How to Talk So Kids Will Listen and Listen So Kids Will Talk*. Avon, 1982.

Glasser, William. *Schools Without Failure*. Harper and Row, 1975.

Glasser, William. *Positive Addiction*. Harper and Row, 1985.

Glasser, William. *Control Theory in the Classroom*. Harper and Row, 1986.

Gordon, Thomas. *Teacher Effectiveness Training*. Longman, 1977.

Gregorc, Anthony. *An Adult's Guide to Style*. Gabriel Systems, 1986.

Harris, Thomas A. *I'm O.K.--You're O.K.* Avon, 1982.

Hart, Leslie. *Human Brain and Human Learning.* Longman, 1983.

Holt, John. *How Children Learn.* Dell, 1986.

Johnson, D. W. and R. T. Johnson. *Learning Together and Alone: Cooperative, Competitive and Individualistic Learning,* 2nd Ed. Prentice-Hall, 1987.

Kohlberg, L. *The Philosophy of Moral Development.* Harper and Row, 1981.

Nelson, Jane. *Positive Discipline.* Ballantine, 1987.

Rogers, Carl. *Freedom to Learn for the Eighties.* Merrill, 1983.

Case Citations

1. *Meyer v. Nebraska,* 262 U.S. 390 (1923)
2. *Tinker v. Des Moines Independent Community School District,* 393 U.S. 503 (1969)
3. *New Jersey v. T.L.O.,* 105 S.Ct. 733 (1985)
4. *Murray v. Curlett,* 374 U.S. 203 (1963)
5. *Goss v. Lopez,* 419 U.S. 565 (1975)
6. *Hazelwood School District v. Kuhlmeier,* 108 S.Ct. 562 (1988)
7. *Lemon v. Kurtzman,* 403 U.S. 602 (1971)

Legislation Cited

Federal Educational Rights and Privacy Act [20 U.S.C. Sections 1232g-1232i]

Hatch Amendment (P.L. 90-247, Sections 439(a) and 439(b) of the General Educational Provisions Act)

Equal Access Act--Public Law 98-377

Forrest Gathercoal is a professor in the Department of Educational Foundations at Oregon State University, where he has taught law for educators for more than twenty years. He has also taught educational psychology, conducted workshops in educational discipline and school law, served as a consultant to school districts across the country, and as a presenter at many educational conferences. Previously at the public school level he has been a classroom teacher, coach, and high school vice-principal, while at Oregon State University he has been director of the placement office and assistant dean of the School of Education. He holds two degrees from the University of Oregon, a bachelor's degree in music and a J.D. from the School of Law. In addition to *Judicious Discipline*, he is a co-author of *Legal Issues for Industrial Educators* and has written numerous articles on educational discipline and school law.

Mr McGregor was planting out young cabbages but he jumped up & ran after Peter waving a rake & calling out 'stop thief'!

and the other shoe amongst the potatoes. After losing them he ran on four legs & went faster, so that I think he would

Peter was most dreadfully frightened & rushed all over the garden, for he had forgotten the way back to the gate.
He lost one of his shoes among the cabbages

have got away altogether, if he had not unfortunately run into a gooseberry net and got caught fast by the large buttons on his jacket. It was a blue jacket with brass buttons, quite new.

'Now, my dears', said old Mrs Bunny 'you may go into the field or down the lane, but don't go into Mr McGregor's garden.'

Mr McGregor hung up the little jacket & shoes for a scarecrow, to frighten the black birds.

Flopsy, Mopsy & Cottontail, who were good little rabbits went down the lane to gather blackberries, but Peter, who was very naughty

Peter was ill during the evening, in consequence of overeating himself. His mother put him to bed and gave him a dose of camomile tea,

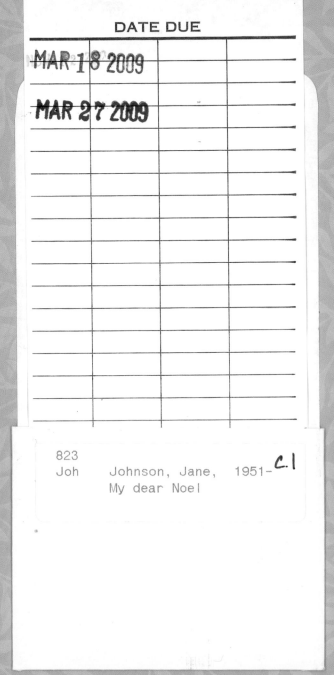

A Note About the Endpapers

The front endpapers are a facsimile of the original picture letter sent by
Beatrix Potter to Noel Moore in 1893. The back endpapers show this same letter but
cleaned for greater legibility and laid out in the correct reading order.

JANE JOHNSON

My Dear Noel

The Story of a Letter from Beatrix Potter

Dial Books for Young Readers New York

For my mother

Published by Dial Books for Young Readers
A member of Penguin Putnam Inc.
375 Hudson Street • New York, New York 10014

Copyright © 1999 by Jane Johnson
All rights reserved • Designed by Nancy R. Leo
Printed in Hong Kong on acid-free paper
First Edition
1 3 5 7 9 10 8 6 4 2

Library of Congress Cataloging in Publication Data
Johnson, Jane.
My dear Noel : the story of a letter from Beatrix Potter / Jane Johnson.—1st ed.
p.   cm.
Summary: A letter from Beatrix Potter to a young friend who is ill marks
the origin of her famous tales.
ISBN 0-8037-2050-5 (tr.)—ISBN 0-8037-2051-3 (lib. bdg.)
1. Potter, Beatrix, 1866–1943—Correspondence—Juvenile literature.
2. Women authors, English—20th century—Correspondence—Juvenile literature.
3. Women artists—Great Britain—Correspondence—Juvenile literature.
4. Moore, Noel—Correspondence—Juvenile literature.
[1. Potter, Beatrix, 1866–1943. 2. Moore, Noel. 3. Letters.]   I. Title.
PR6031.072M9 1999   823'.912—dc20   [B]   96-11074   CIP   AC

The author gratefully acknowledges Judy Taylor's book Letters to Children,
published by Frederick Warne, 1992, for its invaluable information regarding the Moore family.
The art was rendered in pen-and-ink and watercolor.

"Miss Potter's coming today!" shouted Noel as he tumbled out of bed to tell the others.

All the Moore children loved Miss Potter's visits. But Noel had known her longest, so he felt she belonged to him more than to Eric or Marjorie or Freda.

She spent so many hours alone in her room at the top of a big silent house that Noel was sure Miss Potter had much more fun with his family.

"Mama, is Miss Potter having *her* breakfast now?" Noel asked.

Before she could answer, the others began: "Will she bring her mice?" "I want to stroke her rabbit!"

"Wait and see; and don't all talk at once, dears."

When Noel had finished lessons with Mama, Nanny fetched the children's hats and they all streamed through the garden gate onto the common.

I must find something to give Miss Potter, Noel thought.

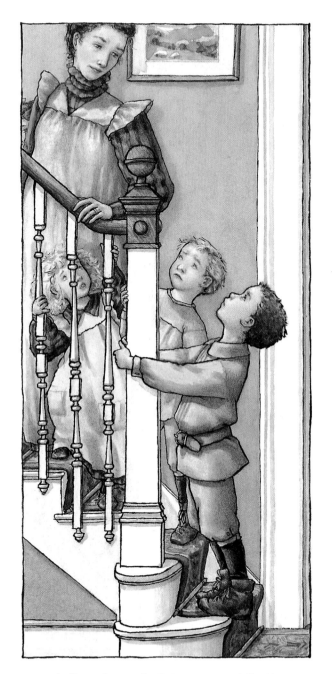

After lunch Mama said, "Now we'll have a rest before Miss Potter comes," and though they fussed, she bundled everyone up to bed.

As Noel's eyes closed, he murmured, "Miss Potter's on her way."

"Oh, it's *lovely* to see all of you!" cried Miss Potter, running up the path. "Is this for me, Noel? What a wonderful color. I shall wear it in my hat."

Then, opening Miss Potter's packages, they discovered treats for everyone—even the new baby who had not yet arrived.

Miss Potter's rabbit, Peter, and her mice forgot the tricks she'd taught them and were naughty instead.

Miss Potter laughed, the children shrieked, and no one scolded.

She told jokes that made
them ache with giggles.
   She drew pictures and never
said, "I'm tired, that's enough!"

Later, when Noel had Miss Potter to himself, she whispered, "I am going to Scotland soon, so I shan't see you for a while. But I *shall* write."

When the time came, Noel could hardly bear to see Miss Potter go.
After a last good-bye, Mama said, "Now, I expect you all to tidy up."
"I'm hot, and my head hurts," grumbled Noel.

"It might just be the excitement, and too much cake," said his mother anxiously.

But in the morning Noel was worse, and because he was often ill,
he knew he'd have to stay in bed a long, long time.

Slowly the days dragged by. Gazing out of the window, Noel listened to the sounds of breakfast, lessons, and then the shouts on the common as the others played.

"Miss Potter would know how to cheer him, Mrs. Moore—I'm kept so busy with the younger ones," said Nanny.

"And I'm worn to a rag with Baby," replied Mama.

All summer long Noel lay in bed, forgetting how it felt to be well.
Sometimes he cried when no one heard him call. Sometimes he slept.

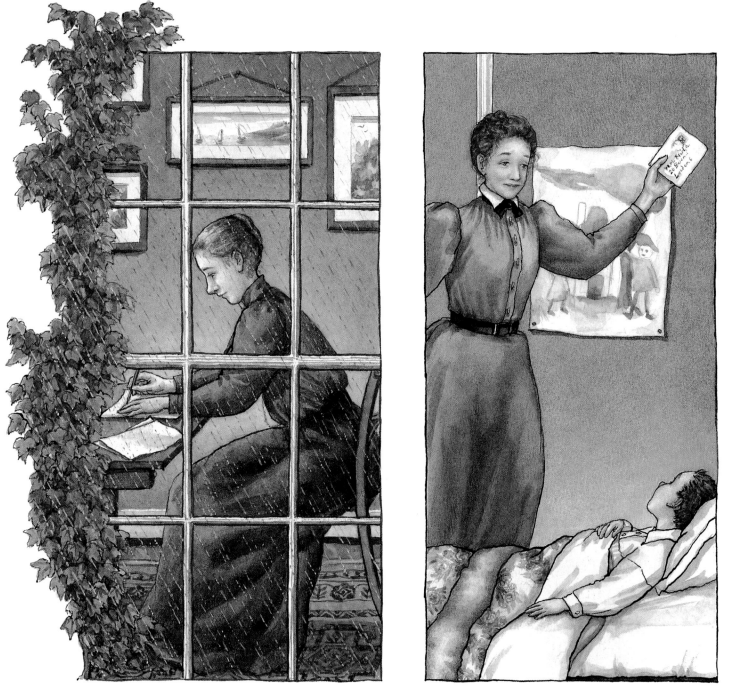

At last, with autumn in the air, a letter came for him.
"See, darling, a fat envelope, full of Miss Potter's news."

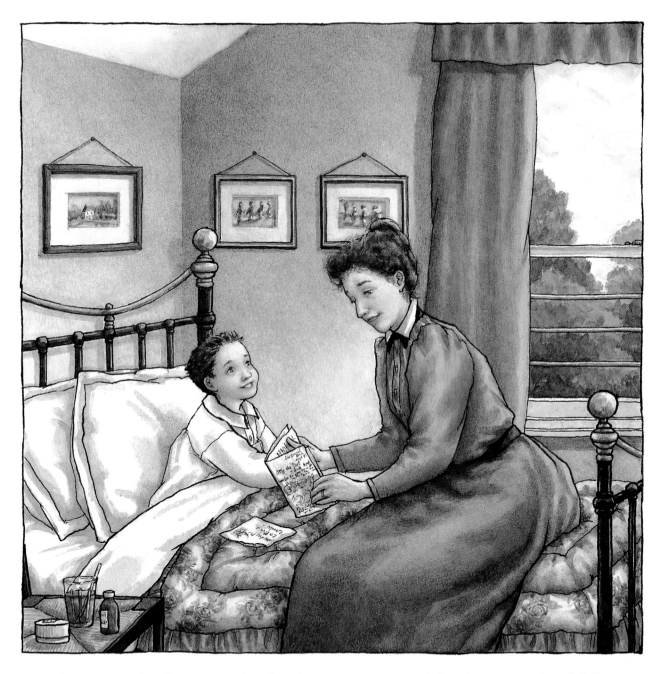

But instead of news, she had sent a *story,* with pictures. And Mama stayed, reading it over and over until she was hoarse.

"It's about a rabbit family, but it's just like ours!" exclaimed Noel as the tale began with a mother rabbit and her children. Then, listening to the adventures of the hero, Peter Rabbit, he decided, "It's really about *me*!"

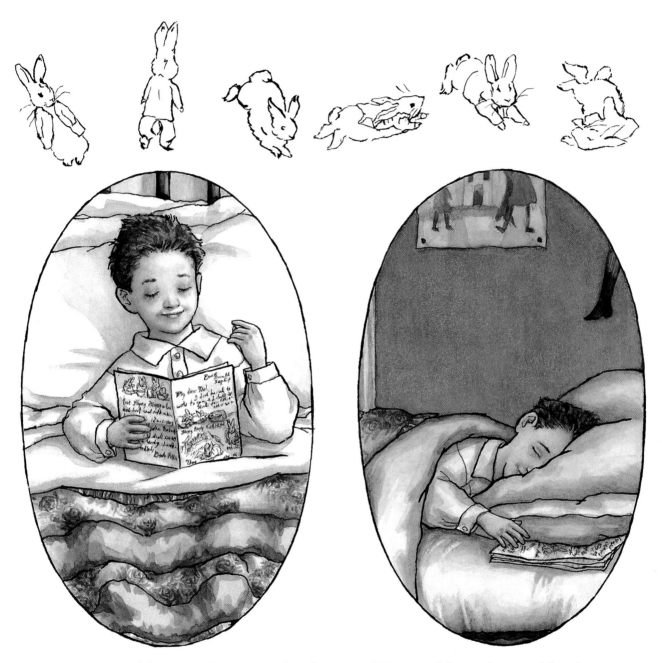

Soon Noel knew the story by heart. He read it to himself whenever
he was lonely. It made him laugh. At night he dreamed that he was
Peter Rabbit, and woke remembering how it felt to run. He wanted to
be well.

Within a week he was getting better, and Miss Potter was back.

"You made that story up specially for me?" Noel's eyes grew dark and round as he gazed at his visitor. "Are we best friends?"

Miss Potter smiled. "Of course we are," she said gently. "Best friends."

Noel Moore was a real little boy who lived in London on the edge of Wandsworth Common, a public park. He was five in 1893 when Miss Potter wrote her first story for him. A few years later he was ill again, with polio, and always afterward walked with a limp.

Quite soon there were eight children in the Moore family, and the house was full. Once she had begun, Miss Potter went on writing stories for Noel, Eric, and the babies as they grew.

At length, Mrs. Moore had an idea that the tales might be made into books, for other children to enjoy. Pleased with this thought, Miss Potter asked if Noel had kept the very first one. And Noel, who had treasured it for seven years, lent her his letter. With the story made longer, and with new, colored illustrations, *The Tale of Peter Rabbit* was published in 1902.

Although Miss Potter's stories made her famous, she never forgot the Moores, who had been her friends when she was lonely and unknown. Noel grew up to become a priest, helping children in the slums of London, and was working among young people at the end of his long life.

Children still read the tales of Beatrix Potter. Perhaps she would never have written them if she had not once known and understood a little boy who needed her. Though far from him, she found the way to reach him, and to reach children all over the world.

Eastwood Dunkeld
Sep 4th 93

My dear Noel,
I don't know what to write to you, so I shall tell you a story about four little rabbits whose names were—

Flopsy, Mopsy, Cottontail

and Peter

They lived with their mother in a sand bank under the root of a big fir tree.

"Now, my dears," said old Mrs Bunny "you may go into the field or down the lane, but don't go into Mr McGregor's garden."

Flopsy, Mopsy & Cottontail, who were good little rabbits went down the lane to gather blackberries, but Peter, who was very naughty

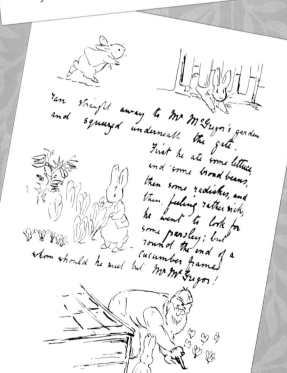

ran straight away to Mr McGregor's garden and squeezed underneath the gate.
First he ate some lettuce, and some broad beans, then some radishes, and then feeling rather sick, he went to look for some parsley; but round the end of a cucumber frame whom should he meet but Mr McGregor!

Mr McGregor was planting out young cabbages but he jumped up & ran after Peter waving a rake & calling out 'stop thief'!

Peter was most dreadfully frightened & rushed all over the garden for he had forgotten the way back to the gate. He lost one of his shoes among the cabbages